STEPHEN JONES &

PETER ASHWORTH

DAVID BAILEY

ANDREW BOLTON

PAUL BOUDENS

HAMISH BOWLES

GEERT BRULOOT

JUDITH CLARK

ORIOLE CULLEN

KAAT DEBO

BARDO FABIANI

JOHN GALLIANO

MAGDALENE KEANEY

NICK KNIGHT

PENNY MARTIN

SUZY MENKES

JEAN-BAPTISTE MONDINO

ANNA PIAGGI

PAOLO ROVERSI

LUCA STOPPINI

SØLVE SUNDSBØ

JUERGEN TELLER

MARIO TESTINO

DITA VON TEESE

STEPHEN JONES
& THE ACCENT OF FASHION

ACC EDITIONS

Stephen Jones for Jean Paul Gaultier, S/S 1984. Picture appeared in *Hanatsubaki* magazine #532, published by Shiseido, 1994.

CONTENTS

STEPHEN JONES & JOHN GALLIANO

John Galliano
Artistic Director of Christian Dior Couture and John Galliano

It is my pleasure to introduce you to this exhibition of Stephen Jones's work, collaborations and fashion friendships.

I have always been a great millinery aficionado, always loved hats and always admired those who create them.

Stephen Jones has worked with me at John Galliano, Givenchy and now Christian Dior for nearly 20 years. We both possess a passion for millinery and his expertise interprets some of our wildest dreams. Each season I travel to new worlds and explore new ideas, and those ideas need hats. Once the design process begins I explain the concept and story behind the collection to Stephen then watch as he develops new shapes and toiles. He understands my style and shares a similar aesthetic; our reference points stem from English backgrounds and a love of history. Ideas bounce to and fro between London and Paris until we have the perfect crown to complete the form we are innovating.

Fashion is a form of expression, empowerment and escapism so I want every detail to enhance my muse. My role is to create and inspire dreams; my duty to enhance every asset and desire, and infuse each season with new energy. Fashion is how we identify our personality, attitude and style – it is what makes us unique, as well as what helps us blend in. I aim to seduce kindred Galliano spirits with new ideas and dress them mind, body and soul. Fashion has the power to speak without words so in each and every collection I push my team to perfect even the smallest of details. I have to make sure that everything, from the inspiration and silhouette to the collaborators I work with, reflects my passion, and, of course, I choose only the best.

This exhibition is subtitled *The Accent of Fashion*, an apt description for the function that millinery performs so well. From fascinators to fascinating, hats need to catch your eye just as much as they need to serve a purpose and complete the outfit you are wearing. Over the years, Stephen and I have created an astonishing range of hats and developed a creative short-hand, and friendship, that is built on trust and mutual admiration. The

Stephen Jones & Nick Knight
Portrait of John Galliano,
wearing armour made by Stephen Jones for Christian Dior Haute Couture, A/W 2007–08.
Archives Nick Knight, *French Vogue* N°873, December–January 2006–07.

complement between fashion and accessory is seen time and time again in my collections on the runway. Hats are as important as a great shoe or bag, and for each collection the partnership between elements must be fresh, new and always relevant to the spirit I am creating. I don't want any hat – I want the right hat. In fittings our creative conversation explores all the options until we select the winning style. Stephen never gives up. He knows how to create a Galliano hat or a Dior hat and make it the perfect hat – that is what is important and sets him apart.

Fashion needs wit, imagination and artists to bring ideas to life. I am fortunate to have Stephen as part of my team and to have him on this wonderful journey with me. In my collections we have adventured through cultures and icons, past and present and around the globe. He knows that I am on a quest for perfection and beauty, and he takes up the challenge down to the very last detail, including the final tilt of a hat 'just so'.

A hat can be a veil or an alibi, a head turner or a friend. It can give clues, or, like this foreword, serve as the introduction to all the wonder that lies within.

Enjoy!

Stephen Jones for Christian Dior
Prêt-à-Porter, A/W 2007–08
Hat in raffia, burnt ostrich and velvet.

Wash'n'Go, S/S 1993. Hat made from resin, imitating water.

STEPHEN JONES & HATS

Stephen Jones
Milliner

In language an accent never sits by itself; instead it adds intensity, prominence or emphasis to a letter. For 30 years much of my work has been about accenting something or someone else. I firmly believe that all artistic creation is based on (and sometimes even in spite of) one's character. Maybe mine was never assertive enough to build my own language of fashion, for I have always preferred collaborating with others to create the final fashion effect. Among the very first hats I ever made were hats for particular people, particular times, particular places: a navy straw trimmed with white asters for my mother to wear to church on Easter Sunday; or a gold skullcap mask for Steve Strange to wear to the Blitz nightclub in Covent Garden, London. Of course these hats fulfilled my artistic expression, but for me meeting the brief was just as important as expressing my ego.

I never wanted to change the world with a hat. I came to London in 1976, the year of punk, when other people were trying to do just that with fashion; so why need I? I had to find a different *raison d'être* for my hats. In the beginning, I made hats for my dandified New Romantic friends at the Blitz club. Along with spats, parasols, pince-nez and other sartorial paraphernalia, hats were hugely important accents to our attire. There we wore clothes not because they were fashionable (the kiss of death) but because they formed part of our self-expression — the outfits were rule-breaking, the more exaggerated and unexpected the better; our efforts to stun each other were almost gladiatorial. I was then a student at St Martin's School of Art (now Central Saint Martins). There Fashion meant the orthodox runway looks of Paris and Milan, certainly not London's individualistic 'street style'. (This was years before John Fairchild declared Vivienne Westwood's genius and Anna Wintour championed John Galliano.) As a designer, I was finding it impossible to reconcile club life, fashion school and my love of hats.

Stephen Jones & Peter Ashworth
Kim Bowen and Stephen Jones in a photo-shoot to announce the Stephen Jones shop in Endell Street, Covent Garden, 1980.
Kim Bowen wearing an opera coat and hat by Stephen Jones.

But then, through Steve Strange and Princess Julia, I was introduced to Helen Robinson and Steph Raynor, the owners of PX, a cutting-edge boutique in Covent Garden where Steve worked during the day. Helen invited me to open a bijou hat salon in the shop's basement and gave me two months to make my first real collection (which looking back could be best described as *Space Age Tudor*). Over the next few weeks, I planted myself at my friend Fiona Dealey's kitchen table and began to coax my first collection into being, using moiré and velvet from Borovick Fabrics, felts from Oxfam, and wire from Paul Craig Millinery Suppliers. I even acted as my own fit model since my recently shaved head was now the stock size of 22½ inches. And then... disappointment; upon completion my collection of about 20 draped berets, pleated trilbies and spiralled tiaras seemed strangely dull. Somehow I needed to build into them the pizzazz and drama my hats acquired when worn by my glamorous friends. How to give a headdress the orchidaceous exoticism of Princess Julia? A toque the scrupulous chic of Kim Bowen? A top hat the jet set *jzoosh* of Francesca von Thyssen? A flat cap the assured style of Steve Strange? Or a helmet the sheer inventiveness of Boy George?

Invitation announcing the move to the Lexington Street Studio. Model Paola Pieroni.

Right: *Glamour & Genius*, bicoloured moiré beret, 1980. Illustration by Lee Sheldrick.

Below: Flat cut hat using origami folding technique, S/S 1982.
Courtesy of Anna Piaggi.

The solution to my predicament, and a resulting shift in my design process, came about with help from collaborators. Lee Sheldrick (my contemporary at St Martin's) added grandiose drama with his exquisite illustrations of archly elegant creatures wearing my hats with aplomb. Then — inspired by the archaic naming process at Lachasse, the London haute couture house where I was a millinery intern — my hats were baptized at midnight, the night before the collection's unveiling, with Gerlinde von Regensburg, the queen of London club life, dubbing them with titles such as *Electric Chair*, *Monolithic Ego II*, *Transcending the Unnecessary* and, my favourite, *Phantom Limb*.

This process endowed my hats with personalities that somehow made them zing. And I realized an important lesson – when I made a hat I must invent a complete character too. For me that is the private thrill of building a collection. Through the countless steps in its realization — the initial inspiration and research, the sketching, the '*toile*-ing', the picking of fabrics, the trimming and the naming – each millinery collection gradually develops a personality. Each tells a different story, unreels a different adventure, from the quasi-scientific — *Rococo Futura* featured nylon wire knitted into space age shapes — to the deeply symbolic — *Sunset on Suburbia* reflected the shimmering but sadly fading glamour of Pinewood Film Studios in Buckinghamshire, England.

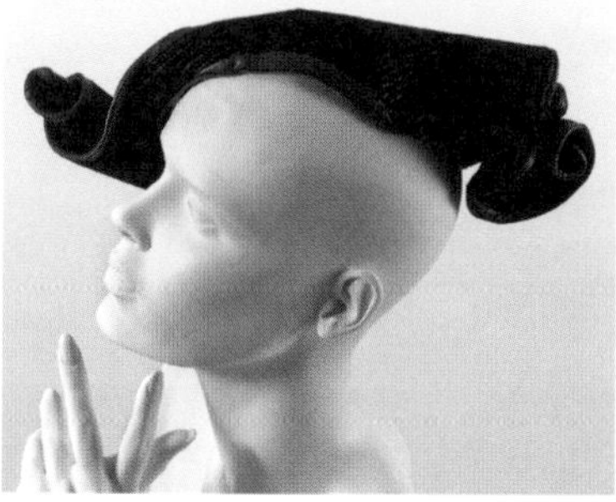

In the modern world of global fashion my private clients seem to appreciate these characters; whether it is Kylie Minogue and me at her home in

Glamour + Genius.
Old Masters.

Top: *Rose Royce*, A/W 1996
A scrolled roseate top hat in black velvet and violet satin. A virtuoso demonstration of the milliner's craft, and one of Stephen's favourites.

Below: Stephen Jones for Giles, Pre-Fall 2010–11

Left: Stephen Jones for Christian Dior Haute Couture, S/S 2010
A classic riding hat in panné velvet and antique veiling by Joscar.

London fitting a headdress of ultramarine ostrich-feathers for her *Showgirl* tour; John Galliano tweaking an haute couture veil on the slickest of my *Wicked Lady* riding hats at the maison Dior on avenue Montaigne; or loyal customer Deborah Quinn visiting the leading Australian boutique Le Louvre to buy *Soho*, a geometric metal trilby, which she will wear to the elegant Melbourne Cup (an Antipodean Royal Ascot). My clients may be just as captivated by the story contained within the hat as they may be flattered by the line of its brim. Often they are looking for another personality, one quite different to their own. Author Jane Mulvagh says she always gets a spring in her step from wearing *Rose Royce*, a tiny scrolled black velvet and violet satin topper, while for Dita Von Teese, a girl originally from Michigan, the coquettish *Geneva* beret in black-lacquered Swiss straw is the essence of European chic.

Designer clients also love the stories and personalities that hats evoke. From the charming familiarity of a straw country hat for Comme des Garçons to the wacky originality of Giles Deacon's photographic print of spinning spanners, hats are the accents of their collections – the exclamation mark that adds variety and personality to each ensemble. A dynamic chapeau can shift the fashion focus. Jean Paul Gaultier, my first client in Paris, loved humour in a hat, be it a crazy fez with a wobbly tassel or pointed turbans to go with his famous cone-breasted dresses. In total contrast, asymmetric vizors and balaclavas (in studded leather for winter and transparent straw for summer) broke the formal symmetry of Claude Montana's cut-with-a-compass tailoring of the 1990s. Nowadays, hats for Marc Jacobs accentuate the season's theme, whether it is cashmere cloches for Roman ladies going shopping or jumbo gem-studded caps to highlight and counterpoint a cocoon-like shape.

Personally I attained 'millinery nirvana' almost 20 years ago when John Galliano asked me to collaborate on his collections. His grammar of fashion is not just extensive but in several different languages! Together with him and his incomparable team, I have been able to accent some of the most fabulous silhouettes in the history of fashion: *Mouth-watering*, a Native American thunderbird made from wooden lollipop sticks, perched atop a slither of a black frilled-georgette dress for the Galliano label; *Himalaya Warrior*, a hill tribe headdress with giant horns, was worn with a crazy multicoloured, multimedia coat for Christian Dior Haute Couture; and *Campus Christmas*, an iridescent lavender trilby made from knitted-paper, finished off a Quentin Crisp suit for Galliano Homme. A hundred memorable creations inspired by bouncing off Galliano's unparalleled imagination flood my millinery memory with bliss.

It was 22 years ago that I first encountered Geert Bruloot, owner of Louis, a cutting-edge fashion boutique that had opened in Antwerp in 1986. My then assistant, Vicki Sarge, sold a number of hats from my 1988 model millinery collection to him, beginning a long-term relationship between Geert and me. My zany hats were the perfect foils to the avant-garde *Antwerp Six* fashion designers stocked at Louis, who were then taking the world by storm. That first collection Geert bought from was called *Room Service*, so titled because the ideas for it came to mind during a study trip to the 1950s hotels of Miami Beach. The work of hedonistic architect Morris Lapidus — whose autobiography is fittingly entitled *Too Much is Never Enough* — was particularly inspirational. Among the hats Geert bought was *Champain*, a streamlined top hat that paid homage to a *Jetsons*-style hotel of the same name.

Since then Geert has returned every season to find his favourites — hats of adventure with slices of science, dustings of glamour, or rococo flourishes. Over the years, he has amassed the largest collection of my hats in the world, a collection which now forms the core of the exhibition here at MoMu, Antwerp's fashion museum, and this glorious accompanying book.

Bravo Geert! Bravo Antwerp! Bravo chapeaux!

Top: *Champain*, A/W 1988–89
MoMu Collection B02/24

Bottom left: *Vogue UK* cover, February 1995.

Portrait of Stephen Jones, wearing *Wild Street*, A/W 2008–09.
Hats from left to right: *Evadne*, A/W 2006–07; *Anna P*, S/S 2009; *Taxi*, A/W 2008–09; *Electra*, A/W 2006–07; *The Women*, A/W 2002–03; *Fire*, S/S 2008, Berlin, 2008.

STEPHEN JONES & THE ACCENT OF FASHION

Kaat Debo
Director MoMu Antwerp

In January 2002, Geert Bruloot and Eddy Michiels, two private collectors from Antwerp, entrusted their unique collection of Stephen Jones hats to MoMu, Antwerp's fashion museum, on permanent loan. They had been collecting hats by the British designer for over 20 years and each season they continue to add new purchases. Now, in 2010, their collection has grown to include no fewer than 122 Stephen Jones hats, making it the largest in the world after Jones's own archival collection. During the research for this book, Jones's team managed to track down Bruloot's very first order slip. Dated 14 March 1988, it records the purchase of eight hats from Jones's *Room Service* collection (autumn–winter 1988–89) for Bruloot's then multi-brand store, Louis, which had opened the previous year on Antwerp's Lombardenstraat, just a stone's throw from the present location of the fashion museum.

Louis was the first Belgian store to exclusively carry collections by Antwerp designers.[1] In 1986, six young Belgians, all alumni of the Royal Academy of Fine Arts, Antwerp, participated for the first time in the *British Designer Show* in London.[2] Convinced of these young designers' potential, Bruloot had organized a stand for them to share and accompanied them on their first trip to London, to help with communications and logistics. The Belgians were immediately noticed by the British press, who – finding their Flemish names difficult to pronounce – christened them the *Antwerp Six*. In 1988, Bruloot accompanied the six designers on their third visit to the *British Designer Show*, where they presented their autumn–winter 1988–89 collections, this time at a group show at London's Westway film studios. The fashion show took place on Friday, 11 March with showroom presentations running 12–15 March. On 14 March, the next to last day of the event, Bruloot ordered his first eight hats from Stephen Jones.

It was not actually a Stephen Jones hat that had first attracted Bruloot's

1. From the first season, as her first customer, at Louis, Geert Bruloot sold collections by Ann Demeulemeester, as well as those of Dirk Bikkembergs, Dirk Van Saene and Marina Yee. In the store's second season, they were followed by Martin Margiela, who launched his own collection under the name of Maison Martin Margiela only one season after his former classmates at the Antwerp Academy of Fine Arts.

2. Dirk Bikkembergs, Ann Demeulemeester, Dries Van Noten, Dirk Van Saene, Walter Van Beirendonck and Marina Yee.

Stephen Jones & Juergen Teller
Special commission, Great Queen Street, London, 2010.

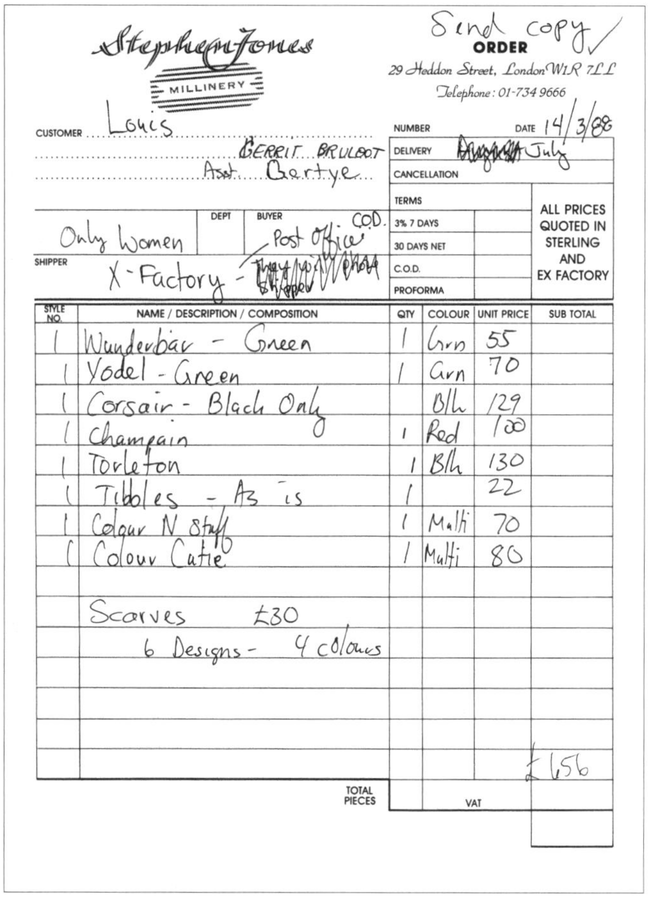

Stephen Jones
MILLINERY

Send copy ✓
ORDER
29 Heddon Street, London W1R 7LL
Telephone: 01-734 9666

CUSTOMER: Louis
GERRIT BRULOOT
Asst. Gertye

NUMBER
DATE: 14/3/88
DELIVERY: July
CANCELLATION
TERMS
3% 7 DAYS
30 DAYS NET
C.O.D.
PROFORMA

ALL PRICES QUOTED IN STERLING AND EX FACTORY

DEPT
BUYER
Only Women
Post Office C.O.D.
SHIPPER: X-Factory

STYLE NO.	NAME / DESCRIPTION / COMPOSITION	QTY	COLOUR	UNIT PRICE	SUB TOTAL
1	Wunderbar - Green	1	Grn	55	
1	Yodel - Green	1	Grn	70	
1	Corsair - Black Only		Blk	129	
1	Champain	1	Red	100	
1	Torleton	1	Blk	130	
1	Tibbles - As is	1		22	
1	Colour N Stuff	1	Multi	70	
1	Colour Cutie	1	Multi	80	
	Scarves £30				
	6 Designs - 4 colours				
					£656

TOTAL PIECES
VAT

Top left: *Fulcrum*, S/S 1998
Balancing on the past and the future, raffia and nylon in a cap-toque.
Tatler, May 1998.
Top right: Geert Bruloot's very first order note, 14 March 1988.

Right: Stephen Jones for Ghost 1993. Outfit by Ann Demeulemeester.
Vogue UK, April 1994.

attention. Three years earlier, in 1985, Bruloot had seen a series of portraits by photographer Nick Knight in the British magazine *i-D*, which included a black-and-white photograph of Jones. Intrigued by this portrait, in which Jones partially hides his face behind one of his own creations, Bruloot set out in search of his work. The portrait that instigated Bruloot's lifelong fascination with Stephen Jones's hats has here been selected for the cover of this book and the poster for the exhibition of the same name.

Although Bruloot's discovery of Jones's *oeuvre* took place against the backdrop of the international breakthrough of Belgian fashion in the late 1980s, it also had everything to do with his passion for all things British. Bruloot had grown up in the coastal town of Ostend, Belgium, where British pop music and BBC radio and television programmes coloured his youth. From the time he was 16, he regularly took the night ferry from Belgium to London.

'A trip to London,' according to Bruloot, 'almost seemed more self-evident than a visit to Brussels. We bought clothes and music – the very latest. Night life in Ostend at the time was completely dominated by London and the British radio DJs. Young people flocked to Ostend from all over Belgium and northern France because we had quicker access to the new music from London.'

As a student in the mid-1970s, Bruloot discovered punk on King's Road:

'Punk was a very strong presence in London and not just in the shadows. Punk was about a lot more than music. It was a way of life that reached into fashion, films and even store design. I still remember SEX, Vivienne Westwood's store on King's Road, later reopened as World's End. The floor in World's End has a sloping surface so the clothes hang on the racks at an angle and outside on the facade there is a clock that ticks anti-clockwise. Westwood herself spoke to us, clothed in one of her own designs – the 'mini-crini' [a cross between a 1960s mini-dress and a 19th-century crinoline] – and high platform shoes. That store was a trailblazer. I have never seen anything like it.'

Bruloot also admits that he is fascinated by Jones's dandyism.

'When I talk about a dandy, I don't mean exuberant taste in clothes or anything like that. The dandy in Stephen Jones is in his versatility, his wide range of taste. Stephen's creativity knows no bounds. He combines that freedom with an unparalleled capacity for putting himself in perspective. You often find that quality in people with exceptional talent, people with multisided creativity. Stephen has no fear of betraying his own image, of breaking away from what has gone before and carving out a completely new path. I see a similar ability to put one's self in perspective in the *oeuvres* of people like Alfred Hitchcock or Martin Margiela.'

Top: Sketch for the *Jordan* turban. Jordan was Vivienne Westwood's shop assistant in SEX and her silver beehive was one of London's landmarks in 1976.

Bottom: *Jordan*, satin turban inspired by Jordan's hairdo and felt eyepatch evoking the cartoon call outs in the work of pop artist Roy Lichtenstein, A/W 2003–04.

Right: Alan Jones, Chrissie Hynde, Jordan and Vivienne Westwood, 1975. When Stephen Jones was a student at St Martin's in 1976, Chrissie Hynde was one of the models in the life drawing class.

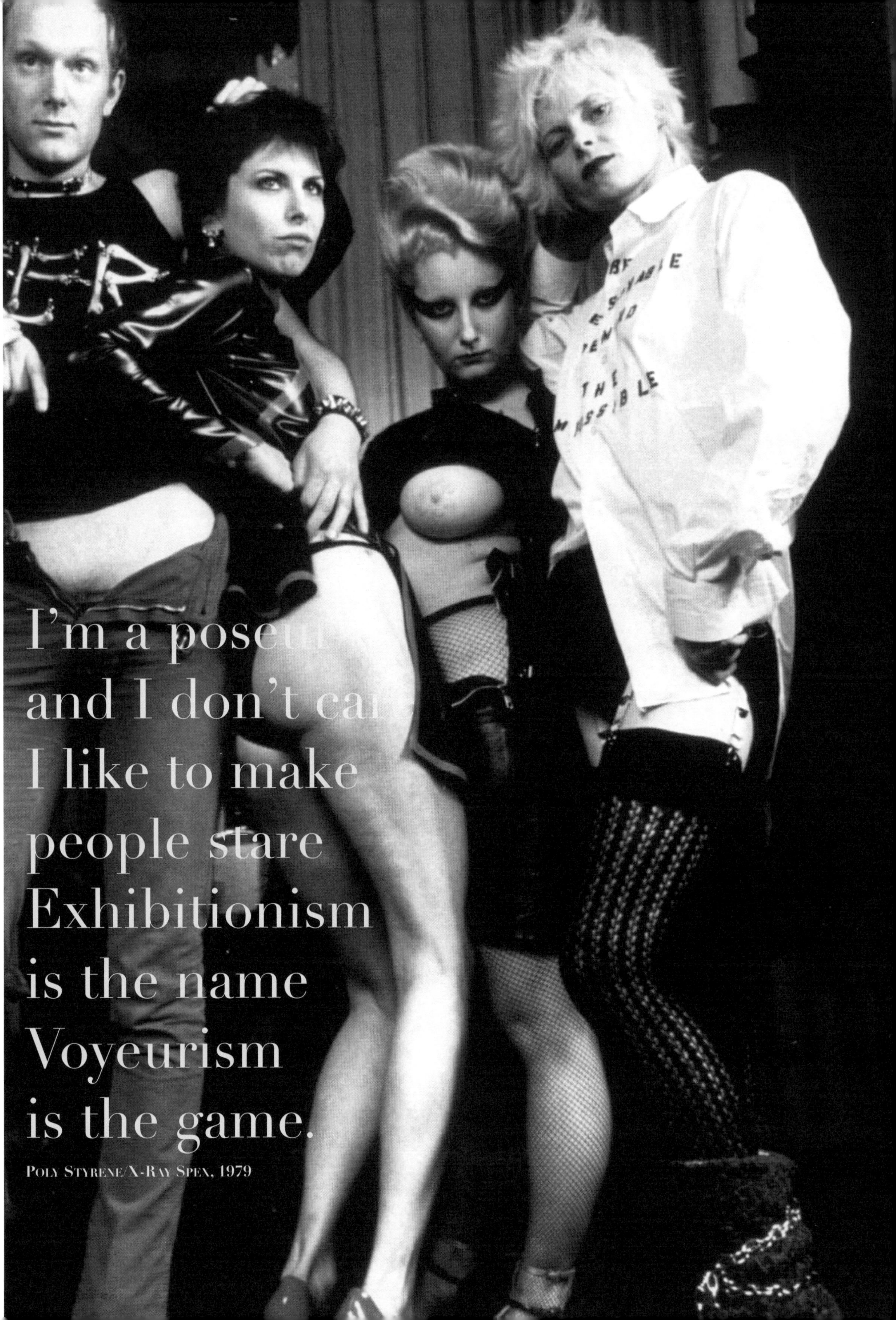

I'm a poseur
and I don't care
I like to make
people stare
Exhibitionism
is the name
Voyeurism
is the game.

Poly Styrene/X-Ray Spex, 1979

Although Bruloot initially purchased Jones's hats to sell in Louis, by the end of the first season his sales had failed to meet expectations; it was proving difficult to convince Belgian customers to wear hats. Indeed, in Belgium the hat culture had long since disappeared. Up to World War II, wearing hats was an integral part of social etiquette, and millinery shops were a common sight on Belgian streets. The many cardboard or leather hatboxes conserved in the MoMu archives are silent witnesses to the millinery shops once found in the centre of Antwerp, which virtually all closed their doors over the course of the 20th century.

The demise of the etiquette and social status that for centuries went hand in hand with wearing head coverings slowly but surely contributed to the loss of Belgian hat culture. During World War II, many women were obliged to work outside the home for the first time. Their professional activities led to increased status and new freedoms, which would never be given up once the war ended. Women suddenly had less free time and needed a practical wardrobe to suit their careers. The formalities intrinsic to wearing hats no longer seemed consistent with their developing roles in society.[3] Great Britain experienced a similar evolution but traditional class consciousness meant that, unlike in Belgium, a greater affinity for hats and wearing hats continued to survive. Today, the British social agenda still marks many events — including the annual horse races; Royal Ascot is undoubtedly the best known — where donning a hat is part of a strict social etiquette. In recent decades, the British royal family, especially the late Diana, Princess of Wales, played a major role in maintaining British hat culture.

Although Geert Bruloot did not immediately find an enthusiastic clientele for Stephen Jones hats in Antwerp at the end of the 1980s, he continued to place new orders, season after season. The hats were initially displayed in the shop window but they gradually expanded into a valuable, fully-fledged collection. Since Bruloot eventually began purchasing without commercial concerns dictating why he chose this or that hat, over time the collection has come to embrace highly exceptional designs, including a variety of hats that Jones designed for collections by John Galliano. Since the 1980s, Bruloot and Michiels have also collected sculpture, photography and fine art. Their collection now includes work by Cindy Sherman, Robert Mapplethorpe, Louise Bourgeois, Malcolm Morley and more.

'We collect fine art purely for ourselves', explains Bruloot, 'not with the intention of exhibiting it. You live with an art collection; you create a dialogue with yourself. That sometimes means that some works need to be stored away for a while.' Collecting Stephen Jones hats comes from an entirely different perspective, 'to show them, to share them with others and preserve them for the future. This is also the reason why we offered

3. McDowell, Colin; *Hats: Status, Style and Glamour*, Thames & Hudson, p. 160

Talia, A/W 2006–07
Tiara made of plated mouldings used for cabinetry with bead rococo curlicues.
Made by Mutsumi Kinoshita.
MoMu Collection B08/20

the entire collection on permanent loan to the Antwerp fashion museum. We want to make Stephen's creativity and unique oeuvre accessible to the widest possible audience. We only collect work by Stephen Jones, not any other hat designers. His hats are more than just headwear, they are fashion statements. He thinks about the elegance that a hat generates, about the impact that a hat has on the rest of your outfit, your hair, your make-up, your entire demeanour.'

After 22 years of fervent collecting on the part of Bruloot, I invited him to help develop a retrospective exhibition on Stephen Jones as co-curator and exhibition designer. Together, we asked Jones if he would like to work with us on a solo exhibition in autumn 2010, concurrent with the 30th anniversary of his house, Stephen Jones Millinery. We quickly realized that we wanted this exhibition to underscore Jones's unique place in the fashion landscape and the diversity of his oeuvre, with its links to music, film and photography. His life and career read as a long succession of encounters that continue to make new opportunities and collaborations possible.

The terms collaboration and group effort are crucial to a proper interpretation of Jones's work. The ampersand — & — found in the title of this exhibition and book was chosen deliberately. Jones always tries to work inclusively despite the fact that fashion often presumes exclusivity. He believes that it is essential for a fashion designer to believe that the world will dress the way he or she sees it. As a hat designer, he does not feel that need. Each collaboration is like a dialogue in which each partner requires a different approach:

'Designing a hat is like a conversation. I have a different conversation with Rei [Kawakubo] than with John [Galliano]. Translating it in their style is easy. What you have to do is to be able to understand what they are saying to you! You have to be aware of how they are different. If you were making a dinner for Dries [Van Noten] it would be very different from making a dinner for Ann [Demeulemeester]. It is just being sympathetic to the other person. It is also a matter of respect.'

Collaborating with others and sensing or complementing their work — whether they are a fashion designer, musician, photographer or film director — have been important to Jones's career right from the start. After graduating in fashion design in 1979 from St Martin's School of Art, London, he went to Paris to look for work as a fashion designer. After a while, he returned to England with no job and no money, and went to work in his father's company. In the evenings and weekends he devoted himself to making hats for friends, including close friend Kim Bowen. It was during this period that Jones and his friends started hanging out at the

Past Present Future, Stephen Jones for John Galliano, S/S 1997
Inspired by a gypsy's crystal ball.
MoMu Collection B02/27AB

Tina Sparkle, Stephen Jones for John Galliano, S/S 1997
Inspired by the circus and more specifically the typical sparkly girl riding bareback.
MoMu Collection B02/22

Blitz nightclub in Covent Garden, one of many clubs on the London night scene in the early 1980s. It was here that he met members of Spandau Ballet, Boy George — who worked in the cloakroom — and Steve Strange, owner of the club, lead singer for Visage and later Jones's very first paying customer. Jones recalls:

'Whether it was Cerith Wyn Evans as a painter, or John Maybury as a filmmaker, or Leigh Bowery as a performance artist, or [Boy] George as a singer, everybody did push each other. We all supported each other. If someone had an opening, we all came along. It was an unusual time. There were also senior figures in the art scene who were influencing us, like Francis Bacon or Derek Jarman. There was a huge squat in Warren Street. I didn't live there but I had a workroom there. Twelve of our group of friends were living there, including Boy George, [David Holah and Stevie Stewart from] Bodymap, Marilyn and [dancer/choreographer] Michael Clark.'

This was the early 1980s. The previous year, Margaret Thatcher, leader of the Conservative Party, had been elected Prime Minister. The British economy, then all but brought to a halt by countless strikes and massive unemployment, was brought back by the iron hand of the Iron Lady, who used economic policy to weaken the labour unions. In the same period, the New Romantics subculture, an offshoot of, and response to, the raw character of punk and the New Wave scene, was at its peak. For both punk and New Romanticism, the symbiosis between fashion and music was crucial. 'You were completely defined by the music you liked. I remember you had to choose whether you were into Roxy Music or David Bowie. Believing the fantasy was real, which is what David Bowie and Bryan Ferry were about, seemed to be so much more tantalizing. Somehow this was in colour and the world outside was beige, not even as chic as black and white.'

According to Jones, the designer who best embodied this symbiosis was Antony Price, who had designed for Bowie and left his stamp on the looks of Bryan Ferry, songwriter and lead singer of the British rock band Roxy Music. Jones nonetheless emphasizes that for him and his friends fashion was above all a means of personal expression and cannot be compared to today's concept of 'designer fashion'.

'Clothing for us at that time was our personal expression. The idea that it was fashionable was not important. At the Blitz club, they looked down on St Martin's students who were too fashionable. If you bought designer clothes, it was an admission of failure because you couldn't do something better yourself, or you couldn't create something. Our cultural motto was 'We don't need fashion, because we create our own fashion'. We knew Montana and Mugler, and, yes, we thought it was exciting, but it

Top: Stephen Jones on the runway with a tray full of hats, during Jean Paul Gaultier's A/W 1984–85 defile.

Bottom: Jean Paul Gaultier, S/S 1984

was just a thousand miles away. We were in London. They were just doing a different thing: proper, serious fashion business. We were not even tempted to be part of that.'

The clothing style of the New Romantics was especially theatrical, with lots of make-up and accessories, and, consequently, hats as well. Jones made hats for his friends, whose exuberant costumes quickly attracted media attention. He himself was featured in a photograph in the second issue of *i-D*. Launched by Terry Jones in 1980 as an experimental 'fanzine', the maiden issue of *i-D* sported the following announcement: 'Style is not how you wear clothes. Fashion is the way you walk, talk, dance and prance.' Magazines such as *i-D* and *The Face* had no interest in mainstream fashion. Instead they laid the foundations for a new youth culture and a new visual culture. During that same period, the phenomenon of the music video made its debut. Images and the image that such visuals create were suddenly at least as important as the music itself.

In 1982, Jones appeared in the music video for the single 'Do You Really Want to Hurt Me?' by Culture Club, the band set up by Boy George, one of Jones's friends from Blitz. Dressed in a pale blue second-hand three-piece zoot suit and a bright red fez that he had made himself, Jones did not go unnoticed. It would lead to his first design collaboration in 1984, with the French couturier Jean Paul Gaultier. In designing his spring–summer 1984 collection, Gaultier took inspiration from Jones's look in the Culture Club video and invited the milliner to model in his fashion show. A motorcycle accident and a sprained ankle unfortunately intervened.

In the early 1980s, when the mainstream London media would not give a frustrated Jones press coverage because he did not have enough stockists in Britain, he took the advice of his assistant, Sibylle de St Phalle, and once again set his sights on Paris. St Phalle arranged an appointment with Azzedine Alaïa who had just started his own fashion house:

'Sibylle wanted to go to Paris to work. She knew Azzedine Alaïa and I went to see him in the summer. He was fitting a chiffon dress; I think it was on Grace Coddington. He had just left Thierry Mugler and was starting out for himself. Andrée Putman was there too. I showed Alaïa some hats but, as he was not doing shows at the time, he said I should go and see Thierry Mugler. He phoned Thierry and we went to see him. That is what happened the first season in Paris. But because we were going over to see Azzedine, Sibylle had also arranged for me to meet Jean Paul in order to see the film of his men's show. I had my box of hats with me, showed him some and he asked me to do the hats for his women's show. The second season for Gaultier was my real entrée in Paris. I always have a big tray backstage to put the hats in. Jean Paul sent me out on the catwalk carrying

Top: Claude Montana, 1993

Bottom: Claude Montana, S/S 1998
Photographer Norman Parkinson described the headdress looking like 'a deranged flamingo'. Picture appeared in *Collezioni*.

Left: Thierry Mugler, A/W 1984–85
Heavily pregnant Pat Cleveland on a flying trapeze as 'La Madone'.
Halo headdress in embroidered tulle by Stephen Jones.

it. All the girls had turbans on and he had asked them to take their hats off and put them in my tray so everybody would know it was me who had made them. It was Gaultier who presented me to the public. That was a key moment for me and I am eternally grateful to him.'

This remarkable encounter would become the first in a long succession of fascinating collaborations with fashion designers. Over the next three decades, Jones would design hats for all the major names who defined the fashion image of their generation: Zandra Rhodes, Jasper Conran, Claude Montana, Katharine Hamnett, Thierry Mugler, Comme des Garçons, Vivienne Westwood, Jean Paul Gaultier, John Galliano, Walter Van Beirendonck, Giles Deacon, Hussein Chalayan and Marc Jacobs.

On working with designers, Jones comments, 'I think that the designers I work with often want me because of my lightness and my sense of humour, so their designs don't become too self-referential'. In collaborations with designers, it is remarkable that Jones has never restricted himself to any single style or signature but embraces the challenge of responding to their widely differing creative universes. He often works with multiple designers during the same season, which, he explains, demands exceptional concentration and is the reason why he works to a tightly structured, almost mathematical plan. 'I often choose not to get involved too early because it is like a big vacuum cleaner on my brain. In the first stages, ideas can change so fast and so often that it can be a waste to start too early. I sometimes have to protect myself a bit.' Jones's contribution varies from designer to designer. With some, such as Rei Kawakubo of the Japanese house Comme des Garçons, he has more of a sense of breaking into the designer's work and, if needed, to rearrange things. He adds with a smile, 'I get carte blanche until Rei Kawakubo says "No".' With other designers, including John Galliano, it is more about adding to a silhouette or to the collection's image.

In addition to his own collections and his collaborations with fashion designers, over the last 30 years Jones has completed countless assignments for film, music and photography. Each of these disciplines results in a very different collaboration depending on the effect the hats need to achieve. He finds designing hats for films – which have included *Elizabeth: The Golden Age*, *Atonement* and *Coco avant Chanel* – completely different from his work in fashion.

'Making hats for a film is all about detail. If you do a hat for a fashion show, people see it from 20 metres away. When you are doing a film, it is the reverse. If Marlon Brando wears a leather jacket all the way through a film, the design of that jacket is absolutely crucial. All of a sudden, everything depends on it.'

For costume dramas, Jones never simply creates replicas of historical hats; directors approach him because they want his unique and unusual signature. 'The costume can be period-accurate but the hat can be a little bit different to give it a bit more modernity or freshness, or to add a bit more of the character of the person who is wearing it.' The list of musicians and pop stars who have called on the talents of Stephen Jones in recent years is downright impressive: Boy George, David Bowie, George Michael, Mick Jagger, Simon Le Bon, Rihanna, Madonna, P!nk, Christina Aguilera, Kylie Minogue ... 'For a pop star, a hat can be really fantastic because it immediately gives you a specific look.'

For this book, Jones invited several photographers to create an image with one of his hats. They are, once again, the pioneering names of their generation and, from working often with Jones, have been important contributors to the international breakthrough and distribution of his *oeuvre*. David Bailey, Paolo Roversi, Sølve Sundsbø and Juergen Teller created new works for the book while Peter Ashworth, Nick Knight, Jean-Baptiste Mondino and Mario Testino selected photographs from their archives. Each of these photographs introduces one of the essays in this book and can be read as tributes to Jones's impressive career.

In every new collaboration, in each different discipline, Jones and his hats bring a unique accent. This is what the title of the exhibition – *Stephen Jones & The Accent of Fashion* (as suggested by Anna Piaggi, one of Jones's most loyal fans) – refers to. Just as accents in a text can lead the reader to its intended reading, or to pronounce and interpret the text correctly, a Stephen Jones hat brings its own specific punctuation to a silhouette, to the overall image of a collection, a photograph or a film. In language, accents often sit at a 45 degree angle, the angle most often used by Jones when placing a hat on someone's head. For the British, moreover, an accent in text is something rather exotic since they rarely appear in the English language. Jones compares it to the compulsion for adventure and discovery that motivated 19th-century Victorian explorers. For his Stephen Jones Millinery collections, he seeks both the exotic inherent to his own British heritage as well as sources of inspiration that he brings back from his frequent travels – whether to Utah in the American West or to South East Asia. Jones has also shown himself to be keenly interested in the mechanisms that lie at the foundations of all forms of exoticism. He recognizes the humour in translating foreign influences into one's own context or the framework of one's own times. For him, the historical inaccuracies in many fashion designers' works are an endless source of inspiration and lead to the most diverse exercises in style, which are only possible thanks to his almost encyclopedic knowledge of the history of fashion. As he describes it, the style of *Siam Easy*, a hat from his spring–summer 1994 collection,

Top: Madonna in a headdress by Stephen Jones and a corset by Mr Pearl for John Galliano.

Bottom: Headdress and tail by Stephen Jones for John Galliano, for Kylie Minogue's *Showgirl* tour, 2005.

Right: Dita Von Teese wearing *Columbine*, A/W 2009–10.
MoMu Collection B10/33AB

"Stephen understands how the tiny details make the difference between a cute hat and a legendary hat... his chapeaux go far beyond the chic and in fact, become the reference for all others. His work manages to reinvent and redefine, rather than merely carry on the tradition of hat making. There's something special that the masters of millinery from the golden age of hat-wearing knew, and Stephen has that rare talent that sets him apart from any other living hat designer. His joy in his work is visible in each creation."

DITA VON TEESE

Cate Blanchett in *Elizabeth: The Golden Age*, wearing a Stephen Jones crown made out of brass, cut by high pressure water jet, 2007.

Miss World, is 'like a Turkish dress designed by Balmain that still looks like an evening gown from the 1950s'.

Jones's hats often pay homage to designers for whom he harbours profound respect. He designed a range of hats in the style of Cristóbal Balenciaga, for example, as a tribute to Balenciaga's resident hat designer and partner, Vladzio Zawrorowski d'Attainville; the hats included *Christobelle* (spring–summer 1995), *Le Dix* (spring–summer 2003) and *Genie* (autumn–winter 2009–10). Pillbox hats, worn on the middle of the head, are characteristic of Balenciaga. To clarify the balance between hat and clothing in Balenciaga's silhouettes, Jones explains, 'His clothes were quite heavy so it is good to combine them with something small.' In this case, by 'something small', Jones also implies something with a sense of humour. Both *Le Dix* and *Genie* have the typical Balenciaga shape but the former stands out with a colourful feather in Papua New Guinea style, while the latter sports a black bird balancing on its beak in the middle of the hat. 'A hat on top of the head looks pretty heavy. I added the bird for some comic relief.'

The exhibition *Stephen Jones & The Accent of Fashion* is built around four themes: **Adventure**, **Rococo**, **Science** and **Glamour**. In Geert Bruloot's design for the exhibition, each theme is introduced by an enlargement of a hat. These four giant hats have been reproduced down to the smallest detail, including the combs on the insides to secure them to the wearer's hair. The hats are tilted on the floor so that they seem to have been nonchalantly left behind. The objects in the exhibition, both hats and complete outfits, are presented in and on top of enlarged models of hatboxes, which are precise reproductions of those hatboxes used by Stephen Jones Millinery: hexagons in form, lilac in colour, with silver logos. These giant hats and boxes represent the importance of playing with proportions in Jones's work.

Photographs from Jones's own archives have also been a source of inspiration, including an Angus McBean photograph in which Jones appears to be rising out of a hatbox, and a black-and-white photograph of Christian Dior, standing in front of girls leaping from a giant hatbox. The Dior photograph was taken on St Catherine's day when the Paris fashion houses traditionally celebrate their *Catherinettes* — unmarried female staff over the age of 25 — by presenting them with extravagant hats in green and yellow, the colours of St Catherine. The Paris fashion houses still honour this tradition and every year Jones designs hats for the Dior *Catherinettes*.

Each of the four themes in the exhibition can be read as a story in its own right, with individual chapters or subthemes. In this way, we have tried to translate the strong narrative character of Jones's oeuvre into the exhibi-

Invitation for *Forty Five Degrees*, A/W 1989–90.

Anna Piaggi, wearing a Stephen Jones top hat, in an angle of 45°.

FASHION ALGEBRA
D.P.

Right: Stephen Jones for Marc Jacobs, S/S 2008
Toiles of Balenciaga inspired hats.

Left: *Genie*, A/W 2009–10
MoMu Collection B10/46

Dior
TAIGNE

Top: *Bus*, A/W 2008–09
MoMu collection B10/31

Bottom: *Sweetie*, S/S 2003

Left: Christian Dior and the Catherinettes, 1953.

Bottom left: Recent picture of 'La Fête des Catherinettes' at La Rotonde, Christian Dior, Avenue Montaigne, Paris 2007.

tion concept. Jones has detailed narratives to accompany many of his hats, populated with fictional characters who bring the hats to life. One lovely example is *Sweetie*, a hat from his spring–summer 2003 collection, *South*. For *Sweetie* — a bow made from multicoloured tin and trimmed with straw — he imagined the following: 'This bow was made by a maid who worked in the home of Mitzi Newhouse, grandmother of Jonathan Newhouse, owner of the Condé Nast publishing house, somewhere on a tropical island in the South Pacific. She had picked up an issue of *Vogue*, which Mitzi had left lying on the coffee table, and made her own version of the fashion plates in the magazine.'

For *Bus* — a red leather cap from the *Covent Garden* collection (autumn–winter 2008–09) — Jones explained, 'This resembles a cap that would be worn by a bus driver in a popular film, on the back of the head, at a jaunty angle, when a shapely, sexy lady steps onto his bus and distracts him from listening to the racing results. Oh yes — these brass rings in the peak are the headlights of the bus.'

The Stephen Jones collections are often constructed like complex stories in which each hat represents a new chapter. Some collections are motivated by films and Jones will base hats on key scenes; for example, his *Artifice* collection (spring–summer 2007) parallels the story line of *The Red Shoes*, a 1948 British dance film by Michael Powell and Emeric Pressburger. The film is constructed according to the principle of 'a tale within a tale', and introduces a young ballerina — played by the famous redheaded dancer Moira Shearer — who is forced by an unscrupulous impresario to choose between her art — dance — and love. *Life/Art*, a hat decorated with red ballet shoes, clearly references the ballet *The Red Shoes* that Shearer's character dances in the film. *Command Performance* is made from wine-red velvet, like the velvet curtains of a theatre stage. *Ecstasy*, a distorted mask, is adorned with a photograph, a still shot of Shearer's penetrating expression when she is in the delirium and passion of the ballet.

Another tiara, *Fonteyn*, was inspired by Dame Margot Fonteyn, prima ballerina at London's Royal Ballet in the 1960s and dance partner of the legendary Rudolf Nureyev. *Smashed* is a spectacular hat decorated with a star-shaped broken mirror; it refers to the scene in which the impresario smashes a mirror with his fist. *Double Entendre*, made from blue acetate, evokes the various dream sequences in the film. *Nice* is a *Chapeau Niçois* (a flat straw hat) just like those sold at the stall in the station scene: the bow in the centre of the hat is made from a roll of 35mm film. Finally, there is *Corniche*, an open hatbox from which three progressively smaller hatboxes and hats emerge — Jones's wink of the eye to the 'tale within a tale' format of *The Red Shoes*.

Top: Invitation for the S/S 2007 collection, *Artifice*. Illustration by Lawrence Mynott.

Bottom: Invitation for the S/S 2006 collection, *Travelogue*

Left: *Artifice*, S/S 2007 collection
Clockwise from top left:
Life/Art, MoMu Collection B08/1;
Corniche, MoMu Collection B08/3;
Smashed, MoMu Collection B08/9;
Double Entendre.

The first theme in the exhibition is **Adventure**, which is introduced by an enlarged version of *London* from Jones's spring–summer 2006 *Travelogue* collection. This top hat of dark blue artificial straw is decorated on the back with three photographic panels of passport pages. The pages were photographed from Jones's own passport and show visas for the United States, Japan and Israel. The design for this hat was inspired by the film adaptation of Jules Verne's novel *Around the World in Eighty Days*, in which the protagonist, Phileas Fogg, begins his voyage around the globe from a phone box in London. The hat's front bears a coat of arms with the Latin text *ex corona ad astra* (from the crown to the stars) and the heraldic figures of an owl and a rabbit, references to materials often used in making hats, such as bird feathers and rabbit fur that is processed into felt. The crest moreover features Jones's own initials, together with a needle, a thimble and a wooden hat mould.

The theme of adventure delves into hats and collections that reference places, cities and countries, and Jones's countless travels, including, for example, the *Shangri-La* collection (autumn–winter 2007–08), completed after a trip to Tibet, and the *Desert Rose* collection (spring–summer 2008–09), following a stay on a ranch in Utah. This theme is about travel, both in time and in geographical space, with its last stop back home to feature, with a collection inspired by Covent Garden, the London neighbourhood where Jones's store is located. Adventure and travel also imply flight and speed, so here we also present hats inspired by wings, including *Gemini*, *Mercury* and *Seagull*, as well as hats embellished with the most surprising feathers and plumes, and even whole birds, including *Polly*, *Velocity*, *Chi Chi* and *Icarus*.

London, S/S 2006. MoMu Collection B08/16

ADVENTURE

Shangri-La collection, A/W 2007–08
Dharma, MoMu Collection B08/7; *Tivoli*, MoMu Collection, B08/4; *Sikkim*, MoMu Collection B08/5

Desert Rose collection, S/S 2008
Honey, MoMu Collection B08/13; *Earth*, MoMu Collection B08/12; *Air*, MoMu Collection B08/11

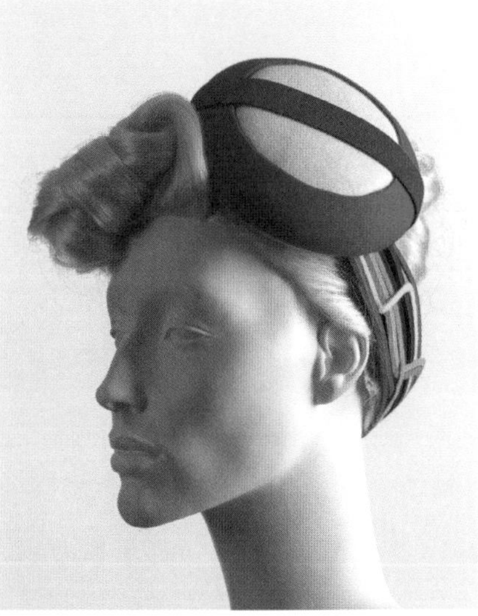

Covent Garden collection, A/W 2008–09
H.Q., MoMu Collection B10/36; *Tube*, MoMu Collection B10/30; *Taxi*, MoMu Collection B10/29

Georgina Stojilkovic models Stephen Jones's cellophane veil for Christian Dior Haute Couture, A/W 2010–11

evian

Top: *Seagull*, S/S 1996
Made from grosgrain.
MoMu Collection B02/58

Bottom: *Velocity*, S/S 1998
The underbrim is made from shards of colour photocopies on acetate.
MoMu Collection B02/40AB

Ladies Day, S/S 1999
Wing made from goose feathers
MoMu Collection B02/50
Image published in *Citizen K* #12, Autumn 1999.

ROCOCO

Bali-Hi, S/S 2002
Created on a block originally used for Grace Kelly by the milliners Rudolf of London. Pleating by Hannah Smith.

The **Rococo** theme is introduced by an enlarged version of *Damn That Feels Good!* (autumn–winter 1999–2000), an asymmetrical hat decorated with an arch-shaped structure of jumbled wood and twigs. The cap, to which the structure is attached, is made from hatter's plush, a silk material traditionally used by hat makers for bowler hats. Jones acquired this specific hatter's plush following the bankruptcy of the firm Rayne, which had been a supplier to the British royal family. The hat's name is a play on words since the hat's shape is reminiscent of a beaver dam.

The term rococo comes from the French word *rocaille*, an 18th-century asymmetrical shell motif frequently applied to French interiors. A great many of the hats in this section take us under the surface of the sea, into a world full of shells, anemones and coral. *Sway* (spring–summer 1999) is an elegant little hat in pleated silk, decorated with two coral branches made of raffia and trimmed with small pieces of pink coral. *Venus*, *Minaudière*, *Black Pearl* and *Engagement* are decorated with shells in every imaginable shape and colour while *Superior* is a black leather tiara with three plastic spheres in the form of sea urchins. 'This hat makes you superior', laughs Jones, 'because people don't get close enough to kiss you. The sea urchins see to that.'

For Jones, sources of inspiration can be exceptionally specific. *Bali-Hi* refers to a style popular in 17th-century Netherlands that was inspired by all things auricular, particularly the waving forms and lobe-shaped curves of the human ear. This style is primarily seen in the work of gold and silversmiths in the first two decades of the 17th century and, in all probability, also influenced rococo and art nouveau ornamentation. Jones has translated this source into an elegant little hat with a complicated pleated structure that drapes over the hat's base in waving movements. In Jones's view, rococo is a 'more lyrical, more charming and more individual style than baroque and is largely concerned with the asymmetry in nature.' Leaf and flower motifs are plentiful in Jones's work, and here and there nature is even literally his *matière première*, as in the case of the bamboo leaves in *Kona Ka'ï* or the wood in *Damn That Feels Good!*. The Rococo theme, however, is also 'about the fluid movements of the brush', as in the hats *Campari & Soda*, *Monday*, *Abstract* and *Rose Royce*.

Damn That Feels Good!, A/W 1999–2000
Inspired by the construction of a beaver's dam, seen on a trip to Lac L'Achigan, Montreal, Canada.
MoMu Collection B02/53

Left: *Superior*, S/S 2001
Tiara with sea urchins made from acetate.
MoMu Collection B02/72

Right: *Glyndebourne*, S/S 1999
Tiara with a branch of silk apple blossom.

Right: *Duplex*, S/S 1996
Monstera Deliciosa plant leaf made from singed leather.
MoMu Collection B02/1

Dita Von Teese wearing *Picturesque*, rhododendrons fashioned from cotton piqué with feather leaves. Inspired by the aesthetic of 1940s Californian architect John Woolf, S/S 2004.

Clockwise from top left:
Wave, S/S 2001, MoMu Collection B02/11
Sway, S/S 1999, MoMu Collection B02/26
Campari & Soda, A/W 1995–96,
MoMu Collection B02/33

Right: *Verglas*, A/W 1999–2000
Berries covered with resin, simulating frost.
MoMu Collection B02/2
Image published in *Citizen K* #12,
Autumn 1999.

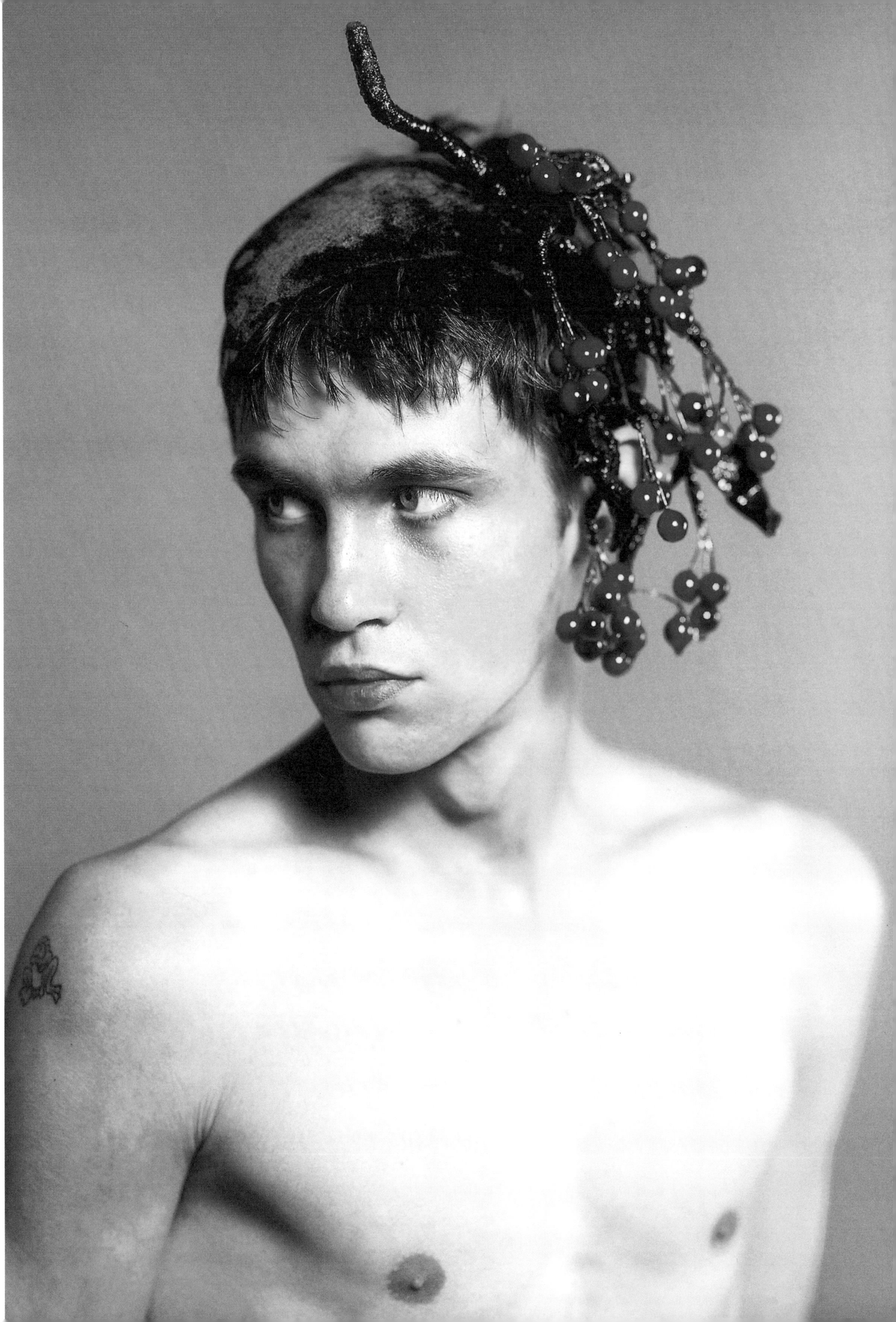

SCIENCE

Formica, S/S 1995
Inspired by 1950s printed Formica evoking architect Oscar Niemeyer's amorphous shapes.
MoMu Collection B02/32

D.N.A.
Image commissioned by Shiseido to accompany the *Rococo Future* exhibition at the Ginza Art Space, Tokyo, 1994.

Science, the third theme in the exhibition, explores Jones's fascination for what he calls the space age and his predilection for science and technology, subjects he already excelled in as a youngster at school. For Jones, science is also about shapes and volumes, varying from a simple line — as in *Hysteric Esoteric*, a tribute to Isabella Blow — to complex cell structures — as apparent in *Aether* and *D.N.A.*.

'I am a typical product of my generation. I'm a child of the 1960s. I always wanted to be a spaceman. The space race was on television and that was modern and exciting. That was the new world. That was the future. People really did talk about the future. At school I was good in a weird mixture of things. I was really good at physics, my favourite subject, and art. The more esoteric and complex it is, the more I love it. And actually that is what I do. It is all about building a bridge. It is about physics. It's about imagining a volume, or a tension, or a colour and making it reality.'

As a small boy, Jones was always good at putting together small mechanical inventions. 'When I was little, I made these machines or mechanisms so I could pull a string from my desk and the curtain would close, or the door would open. Somehow making hats was like making a little machine. It was like making a constructed and solid object, as opposed to making an object by draping fabric around the body — which was a very different thing.' The science theme also covers the many graphic patterns in Jones's work, from elementary rectangles — as in *Alpha*, which was inspired by the black monolith in the opening scene of Stanley Kubrick's science fiction film, *2001: A Space Odyssey* — to two-dimensional designs, such as *AWOL*, a model comprising only the outline of a top hat, and *Gruau*, a tribute to the work of the French-Italian graphic designer and fashion illustrator René Gruau. This theme also reveals Jones's love of architecture with various references to the work of Brazilian architect Oscar Niemeyer. 'The sketched object plays a huge role in Niemeyer's work. You can easily imagine his drawings when you see his designs, the expression of a simple, almost naive movement.'

The hat that introduces this third theme is an enlargement of *Soho*, a classic trilby made of shiny vacuum-formed polyethylene, from Jones's *Millinery Computer* collection (autumn–winter 1998–99). *Soho* is a true classic in his *oeuvre* and its shape has since been reintroduced in various later collections. Jones believes it is an exceptionally pure form, in which he tried to reduce the form to its essence, so that it looks like a sketch for a hat.

Right: *Cork St.*, A/W 1998–99
Hat sculpted from flocked foam.
Cork Street is the epicentre of London's fine art world.
MoMu Collection B02/52

Stephen Jones for Givenchy Haute Couture, appeared in *Vogue Italia* 9/1996. The title of the story is 'Couture Junkyard: Kylie Bax'. Helmet from leather and crin, made by Deborah Davidson, head of the Stephen Jones model millinery workroom from 1983–2010.

Top: *Hysteric Esoteric*, A/W 2000–01
Inspired by fashion icon and renowned hat wearer Isabella Blow.
MoMu Collection B02/84

Below: *Gruau*, A/W 2000–01
Inspired by the mid century master illustrator René Gruau, creator of many Christian Dior images.
MoMu Collection B02/80

Vertical Hold, S/S 1995
Inspired by the 'vertical hold' button on mid 20th-century televisions, to regulate vertical stability.
MoMu Collection B02/13

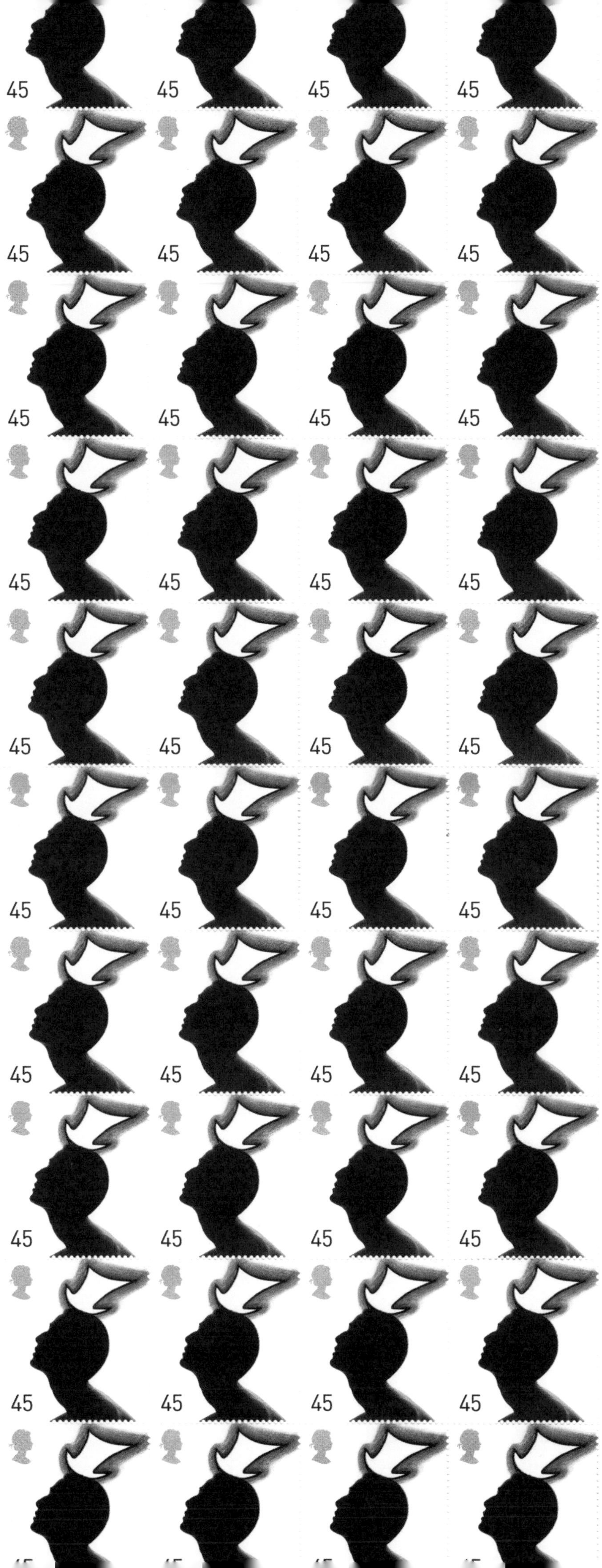

Stamp sheet, featuring *AWOL*, modelled by Erin O'Connor and photographed by Nick Knight; part of a series of spring millinery stamps from the British Royal Mail. A/W 2000–01

Bauhaus, A/W 1995–96
Architecture has always been an important inspiration for Jones. Here the controlled symmetry is rendered in micro pleat taffeta and relieved by silk velvet.
MoMu Collection B02/34

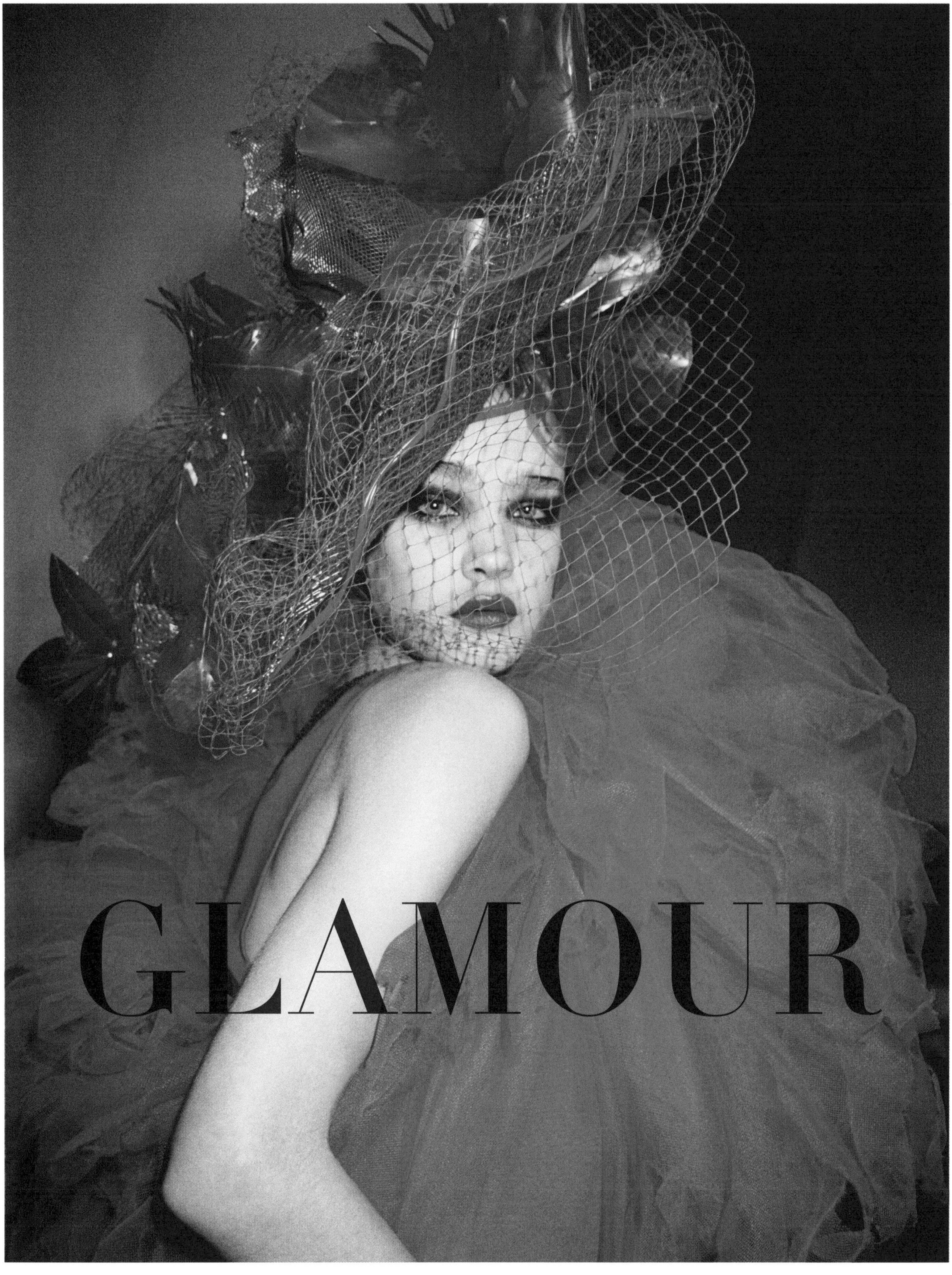

GLAMOUR

Below: Invitation for the *La Prima Donna* collection A/W 2004–05.
Inspired by Duchesa Simonetta Colonna di Cesaro. In the background Simonetta is spied in her leopard trilby, 1962.

Left: Natalia Vodianova smoulders in Stephen Jones for Ungaro, S/S 2003 Portrait hat in wire mesh and tulle and plastic.

Glamour, the final theme, is introduced by a blown-up version of *Ecstasy*, one of the hats inspired by the film *The Red Shoes*. Glamour is about divas, among other things, resulting in a whole array of top hats in varying proportions. *Big Top*, from the Galliano *Circus* collection, is a top hat entirely covered in silver sequins. Traditionally worn in circuses by the ringmaster, the top hat symbolizes power, and, thanks to all the glitter, this version takes on a glamorous tint. *Charade*, from *Murder by Millinery* (autumn–winter 1997–98), is made from rhinestone braid and wire in the contours of a top hat, and immediately brings to mind images of Marlene Dietrich, the ultimate diva in Josef von Sternberg's legendary black-and-white movie *The Blue Angel*. Years later, Jones produced a variation on this hat for another diva: Victoria Beckham.

Glamour evokes sex, parties, boudoir and spotlights. Accordingly, *Ulla* is a tiara made of party souvenirs: a champagne cork, a party invitation and a London Underground ticket. Jones designed *Swing* — a hat referencing the expression 'swinging from the chandeliers' — and *Bubble* — a pink pointed hat in the shape of a classic paper party hat in celebration of the new millennium.

These four themes — Adventure, Rococo, Science and Glamour — take you into the rich imagination of a unique hat designer. It has been an absolute privilege to be allowed a glimpse into Jones's fascinating world over the last few months and I would like to extend my very special thanks to Stephen Jones, Geert Bruloot and Eddy Michiels, as well as to the teams at both Stephen Jones Millinery and MoMu. I would also like to thank graphic designer Paul Boudens, and all the partners and lenders who have made both this exhibition and book possible.

Lose yourself in Stephen Jones's wonderland!

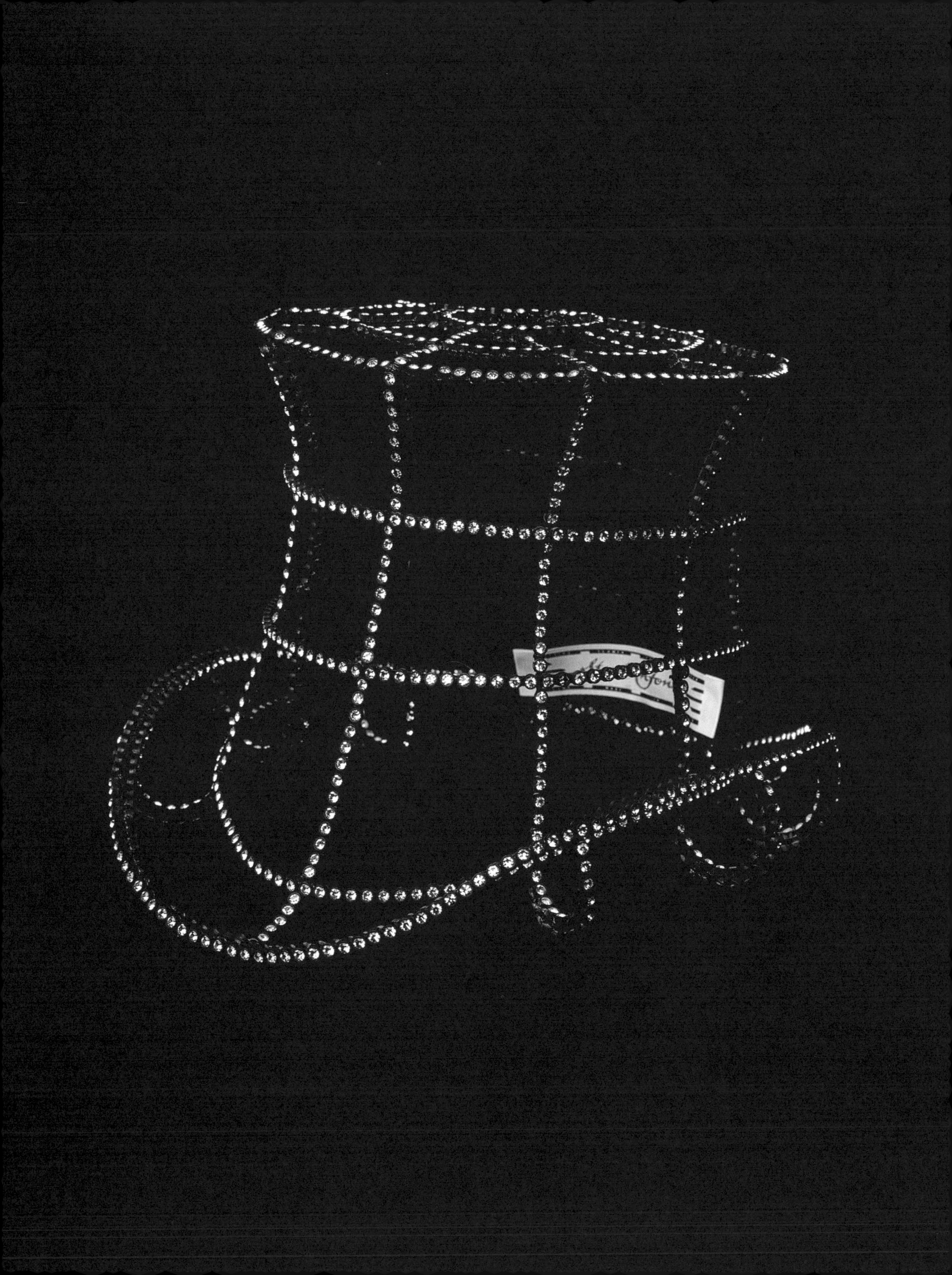

Left: *Charade*, A/W 1997–98. Top hat made from rhinestone braid and wire. MoMu Collection B02/63. Right: Portrait of Stephen Jones, wearing *Carol Channing*. Published in *Time Out*, Jan 10–17 1996.

Top hat made from authentic corsetry fabrics and fastenings. Image published in *Hanatsubaki* magazine #687, Published by Shiseido, 2007.

Pouf, S/S 2009. Hat in ostrich feathers and metalwork by Mr Carel, inspired by a war bride's hat from the collection of the V&A Museum, London. MoMu Collection B10/43.

STEPHEN JONES & THE EARLY YEARS

Hamish Bowles
Editor-at-large, *Vogue*

In 1976, Establishment Britain was reeling from the onslaught of punk, the iconoclastic music and style movement that responded to a bleak decade of power cuts, miners' strikes and governments insensible to the yearnings of the nation's youth. As a student on the Foundation Course at High Wycombe College of Art and Technology, and an alumnus of the prestigious private boarding school Liverpool College, Stephen Jones may have been removed from the travails of many of his countrymen but nevertheless the potency of punk impacted his personal style.

He was, however, unsure of his future and was considering a variety of art disciplines, including ceramic and textile design. Then, in 1976, inspired by the exhibition *Fashion from 1900–1939* at the Victoria and Albert Museum, London, he decided that 'fashion seemed to be the thing that was most lively'. Encouraged by the example of his sister Sarah — who had moved to London and appeared to be 'going to parties and having wild times!' — Jones applied to St Martin's School of Art. The college, centrally located in campuses in Soho and Covent Garden, represented the capital's nexus of fashion and alternative music life. The Sex Pistols had played their first concert there (6 November 1975) and recent star fashion alumni included Katharine Hamnett and Bruce Oldfield. Somewhat to his surprise, Jones was accepted: 'I think because I was a token male — there were only three of us!'

On his first day at art school in autumn 1976, Jones remembers walking into the main room — 'wearing vinyl jeans and a black jumper and chipped black nail varnish' — where the new students had assembled, and being struck by the two distinct groups gathered there. 'In one corner there were all these girls dressed in cashmere', he recalls, 'and a few punks in the other corner. I straddled the two camps so to speak; I did quite like beige cashmere but in a [Norman] Norell swagger-back coat — not a roll-neck sweater! So I went straight to the punks — I thought they were quite charming. The girls in cashmere were intimidating.' He was struck by 'how arch everything was. I'd never really met people who had such a sense of attitude and a sense of self ... it was something that was completely new and strange to me. A lot of them were from London or had done

Stephen Jones & Mario Testino
L'Wren Scott wearing *Baby Grand*, S/S 1988, styled by Hamish Bowles in *Harpers & Queen*.
Archives Mario Testino, 1988.

their Foundation Course at St Martin's so they already had a complete social network going on. We were very much the new people.' Jones remembers being 'obsessed with artifice and otherworldliness. I had grown up watching 1930s and 1940s black and white films on BBC2 on a Saturday afternoon — especially the Bette Davis films when she was always dressed just so. That was really my fashion training up to that point.'
Jones immediately gravitated to a wildly individualistic punk girl named Shanne, who was to become his first art school friend: 'She was wearing her father's black dinner jacket and she had a tampon attached to her lapel and the end of it was colored in red pen. It freaked everyone out and, of course, the cashmere set thought it was completely beyond the pale!' Shanne turned out to be Jones's conduit to a brave new world of contemporary music culture. On that first day, she invited him to join her for lunch in the local Soho market with her boyfriend, 'a toothless Irish charmer' who turned out to be Shane MacGowan of The Pogues, the band that developed its own idiosyncratic hybrid genre of punk and traditional Irish folk and protest music.

Top: Stephen Jones & Hamish Bowles at Katrine Boorman's & Tom Conran's wedding, Glendalough, Ireland, 1989. Jones wearing *Kim* top hat, Bowles wearing *Integrate*.

Bottom: Roxy Music, record sleeve *For Your Pleasure*, 1973. Amanda Lear dressed by Antony Price.

Right: Sibylle de St Phalle & Stephen Jones, both in a Thierry Mugler outfit, in the Lexington Street Showroom. The silver balaclava in the front appeared on the cover of *The Face*, 1986. Picture styled by Frans Ankoné for *Avenue*.

Jones was assigned a room in Ralph West Hall, a Battersea student residence. The occupant of the room next to him, a graphic design student then enrolled at Camberwell School of Arts and Crafts, turned out to be Kenny Morris, drummer of proto-punk band Siouxsie and the Banshees, which had recently been formed. Jones later befriended Sonja Kristina of the group Curved Air, whose drummer, Stewart Copeland, left to form The Police soon after. 'Even in my first year at St Martin's my life was all about music and fashion', says Jones, who notes that at this point the most influential designer of the moment in London was not Vivienne Westwood — the protean talent who gave visual form to the iconoclasm of punk — but Antony Price, a designer whose pulchritudinous creations drew heavily on both mid-century high fashion and comic strip imagery (as Thierry Mugler would later do in Paris). Price was the official designer and stylist for the highly stylized group Roxy Music.

'Fashion and music — at the time we thought that's what Britain had to offer', recalls Jones. 'We knew that no way could we compete with the Parisian haute couture houses like Dior and Chanel. In America, it was Calvin Klein and Halston; it was all so glamorous and Studio 54; and then Milan was about gorgeous fabrics. The thing that gave British fashion its meaning was its link with music.' Before such innovative designers as Thierry Mugler, Claude Montana and Jean Paul Gaultier emerged to energize the Parisian ready-to-wear scene, 'Fashion, per se, was for a different generation — the very Establishment, grown-up world of Venet and Scherrer, Dior and Chanel. Even Sonia Rykiel was working within that French canon of chic — it wasn't exactly street style. Anna Piaggi

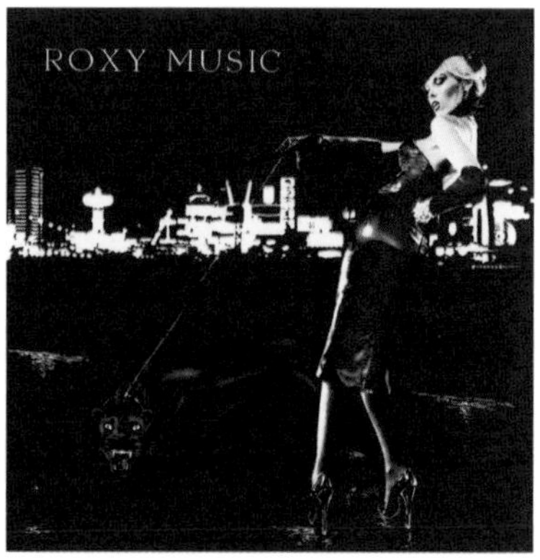

might have been wearing Walter Albini [the glamorously retro-minded Italian designer] but that didn't seem relevant to an 18-year-old Londoner.'

At St Martin's, Jones was studying womenswear but had an antagonistic relationship with his design tutors. Despite the potent influence of the punk movement, Jones felt his teachers were too aesthetically attuned to the vibrant *folklorique* work of Kenzo and a palette of 'bright, happy colours that I really couldn't bear'. He sought refuge in the college library, leafing through the bound volumes of mid-century *Vogue* and finding inspiration in images of Madame Grès' legendary draped gowns: 'I think because I had no technique whatsoever, the most completely complicated technique fascinated me.'

Jones had a happier relationship with one of his tutors, Peter Lewis-Crown. The tailoring instructor kept his classes enthralled with gossipy anecdotes and wryly acerbic observations. He would arrive for lessons dressed in motorbike leathers that when removed revealed his immaculate Savile Row attire. Lewis-Crown was the designer and director of Lachasse, the storied London couture house located in a rambling turn-of-the-century red brick stable block on Mayfair's Farm Street. In the 1920s, the designer Digby Morton, then working for the house, had introduced the concept of the town-into-country tailored suits, creating an ensemble that could serve double duty for its wearer, whether she was stalking the Scottish grouse moors or lunching at the Ritz. It would become a staple of the fashionable British woman's wardrobe. After Morton left to establish his own couture house in 1934, Hardy Amies (later dressmaker to Queen Elizabeth II) replaced him at Lachasse.

Lewis-Crown invited Jones to come work at Lachasse to improve his sewing skills, and so the young student joined the establishment as a summer intern, initially apprenticing to the irascible tailor, Mr Homer – 'pad-stitching collars and picking up pins'. In traditional haute couture style, Lachasse had workrooms specifically for dressmaking (Miss Popham, who ran one of these, had worked for the great pre-war couturier Edward Molyneux), tailoring and millinery. Jones noticed that the atmosphere in the millinery department – adjacent to the tailoring workroom and run by the larger-than-life Shirley Hex – was exuberant: 'There always seemed to be peals of laughter coming from there'. Thinking that he would have more fun working there, Jones asked for a transfer, which was duly granted. 'Hats seemed to be this thing from another planet – a great untapped world with so many possibilities', says Jones. He had also noticed a large pot of glue in the workroom, and assumed, erroneously, that hats were glued together rather than sewn; 'I was dreadful at hand-sewing! Little did I know there is much more hand-sewing in a hat than there is in a dress!'

Left: Kim Bowen wearing a Stephen Jones toque, 1979.

Bottom: Sibylle de St Phalle wearing *Samba Bamba* wiglet, S/S 1984.

Shirley Hex went on to train a new generation of milliners, from Paul Bernstock and Thelma Speirs to Philip Treacy and, of course, Jones:

'She was really a millinery mother with a fantastic sense of humour. I had such a wonderful time there. On day three Mrs Hex said to me "if your hands moved as fast as your mouth does that hat would be finished by now!" The reason I got into millinery was her fun attitude — she played hard, worked hard and was the most incredible milliner, who had been schooled in the most traditional pre-war way and copied Paris models. But she also loved something made out of plastic and spray mount — she had the best of the traditional with a love of the new and she passed that on to both Philip and me.'

Hex's assistant was Miss Lily, an East Ender who chain-smoked while she worked until her snowy hair was yellowed with nicotine.

At Lachasse, faithful clients came in to have their old clothes altered season after season, exemplifying the make-do-and-mend spirit of austerity Britain, which the house and its clients had experienced firsthand. One of Jones's earliest jobs was to 'cut off little pieces from the side seams, piece them all together and make a new trim for the hat'. By day, Jones was working in an antebellum environment with working practices, and even a design aesthetic, that fulfilled a continuum with a court dressmaking tradition dating from the Edwardian era. By night, he was 'pogoing with Vivienne Westwood' and exploring the capital's most avant-garde night-spots where fashion was being created. 'It was this strange dichotomy, really bizarre. But the whole music–fashion thing was the hallmark of Britain.' Nightclubs included The Vortex and Club Louise on Poland Street in Soho. The eponymous Louise 'was a grande dame', Jones recalls, 'a dead ringer for Googie Withers [the distinguished British actress] and she sat at the door with very *soignée* grey hair and a grey mink stole draped low over her shoulders with a Martini and cigarette in its holder'.

Jones trained at Lachasse for two summers, receiving millinery commissions for wedding hats from designer Benny Ong, from Fiorucci, and for a production of *Charlie Chaplin* at the Queen's Theatre in Hornchurch. He began to focus on his St Martin's graduation show in 1979. For this, he presented an ironically anachronistic collection of court presentation dresses (court presentations had been abolished by the Queen in 1958) in white satin and grey *ombré* chiffon, which he remembers as 'late' 1950s, early 1960s punk/couture evening dresses with rather intriguing cuts — I always liked form and control'. The dresses, perhaps prophetically, were accessorized with dramatic headdresses in 'bold geometric shapes that were toque-ish and Egyptian, Nefertiti-esque'; others were accented with platinum-coated coq feathers that Jones had found on a trip to Paris; and then there were 'all these broken tiaras, which were made from triangles of industrial type Perspex, trimmed with seagull wings'. At the time this arch approach was 'really off people's radar — they wanted happy-clappy Kenzo or disco wear'. In fact, his tutors tried to fail Jones, claiming that millinery, which he had chosen as a secondary subject, was not officially recognized by the college. However, the adjudicator, Deryck Healey, an international textile and interior design consultant, insisted that he pass.

Following his graduation, Jones went to Paris for a succession of interviews with fashion houses, including Sonia Rykiel, Jean-Claude de Luca and the fledgling Thierry Mugler, but with no success. His portfolio showed clothes but no hats, as he 'didn't think anyone would be interested in hats!' He returned to England 'with no money' and had to give up his beloved flat in shabby genteel Gloucester Terrace and move out of London (now prohibitively expensive) to stay with his parents in Marlow, Buckinghamshire. There, improbably, he began working for his father's company as a truck driver, distributing fruit and vegetable products. The money he earned soon enabled him to pay off his debts and invest in millinery equipment — 'a *poupée* head, an egg iron and some blocks'.
By 1980, the fashion world had caught on to the arch, retro chic that Jones had embraced in his degree collection. He started to frequent the Blitz nightclub in Covent Garden (introduced by jeweller Dinny Hall) which was a cradle of New Romanticism. Reacting against the iconoclasm and brutalism of punk, the New Romantics — who included Kim Bowen, Stephen Linard and Lee Sheldrick (all first year fashion students at St Martin's when Jones was in his third year) — were inspired both by the transformative quality of David Bowie's persona and the retro camp of band Roxy Music. They embraced a flamboyant aesthetic that referenced such mannered and highly stylized images as mid-century fashion photography and the movies of Federico Fellini. The New Romantics initially congregated at Billy's in Soho for what Jones remembers as 'the first time that anyone had done a club night somewhere. Before that it was just gentlemen's clubs or big discos.'

Jones was profoundly inspired by the fastidiously stylish Kim Bowen, whose exaggerated make-up and coiffure owed a debt to Joan Crawford's 1940s onscreen persona:

> 'I was driving trucks during the day and went home in the evening and set out to make her a whole collection of hats — which she didn't know anything about. She was an extraordinary person and great fun and wore hats extremely well. I made her about ten hats or something ... I remember driving to London to see her. I opened up the back of my minivan, there were all these hatboxes and I said — "Look, I've made these for you!" And she fell off her Maud Frizons!'

Right: *Ritz* magazine (1980) featuring Kim Bowen wearing a Stephen Jones nun's coif in old rose silk. *Ritz* magazine was *the* London society magazine of the early 1980s, with photographer David Bailey as a regular contributor. This session over 8 pages confirmed Jones's arrival on the design scene.

Below: Illustrator Lee Sheldrick, Stephen Jones and Kim Bowen at Jones's salon in Endell Street. Bowen is wearing a shirt from PX and a Stephen Jones hat from the *Hanging Gardens of Babylon* collection. Picture appeared in *So-en* magazine, May 1981.

Magic Inhabited Hat **£60**
Girl **KIM BOWEN**

NIGHTLY CABARET/CLUB
RESTAURA
BAR
LAW SECRETARIES
OPEN

The hats were 'quite strict and very gothic'. In 1979, Bowen informed the *Sunday Times*, 'Hats dictate my outfit'. Jones remembers her wearing them with '1950s trapeze grosgrain coats, which she would wear back to front with a cinch belt on top. Everyone used to call her Archbishop Makarios' (the archbishop and primate of the Cypriot Orthodox Church and the first President of the Republic of Cyprus). Bowen became the iconic female face of the New Romantics and was featured in contemporary magazine coverage on the movement and in the music videos that provided its essential soundtrack.

Jones was making enough money as a truck driver to enable him to give hats to the women whose styles he admired — as well as Bowen, there were Luciana Martinez and (the self-titled) Princess Julia. 'I made them for love! The hats were sometimes extravaganzas but it was the hair and the make-up – everything going together – which made the look,' Jones recalls. In the *Sunday Times*, he cited influences including 'Fragonard, stucco ceilings, [Visconti's] *Ludwig* and [Fellini's] *Casanova*.'

Jones's first formal millinery commission came from Steve Strange (né Steven Harrington), the lead singer of Visage, the quintessential New Romantic group, and, with Rusty Egan, the co-promoter of Blitz. Jones remembers charging £75, an unheard of sum of money, for the resulting creation, which was 'like a skullcap, with a fin on it that came down and swooped over one eye to become an eye patch in black and gold braid'. Strange's skullcap was the first of a number of commissions for the newly established milliner. These hats would soon reach a broader audience, not only through the magazine profiles that Strange relentlessly pursued but also through his group's music videos, including the iconic 'Fade To Grey', and record covers (on one of which Jones himself appears in shadowy silhouette.) By day, Strange and Princess Julia worked as sales assistants at PX, a fashionable clothing store on Endell Street in Covent Garden (an area then still known primarily for its fruit, vegetable and flower markets), which *The New York Times* noted supplied 'the post-punk crowd' with 'new medieval cloaks and tunics'.

Through Strange and Princess Julia, Jones met Steph Raynor and Helen Robinson who owned boutique PX, housed in a 19th-century terraced building. The two invited him to open a salon in the unused basement 'so within one year of leaving college I had my own little shop, which was completely unplanned', notes Jones. He described the shop's aesthetic to *i-D* magazine as 'a boudoir [in a] more "Italian Hollywood" vein with balls' and the hats as 'a cross between Kay Kendall and Casanova ... a reaction against "High Tec" [sic]'.

Top: Vintage crin lurex and chenille braid hat, here modelled by Sarah Leonard. This hat was the first hat Jones sold. It was commissioned by Steve Strange.

Below: The original braid in black and gold.

Top left: The Blitz club, with the band Visage, 1978.

Bottom left; clockwise: Stephen Jones, Sibylle de St Phalle, Barry Metcalfe. Dinny Hall, Lucia and Paola Pieroni, wearing Jones's hats.

Top; at the Blitz club: Vivienne Lynn, model; Boy George, cloakroom attendant; Chris Sullivan, singer; Kim Bowen, stylist; Pinkie-tessa, cabaret artiste.

Below right: Stephen Jones, Patrick Cox, Keith Haring and Boy George at La Coupole, Paris, 1985.

Left: Stephen Jones at Le Beat Route club in Soho, wearing a leather Stephen Jones cap with barbed wire and a jacket made by Boy George, 1982.

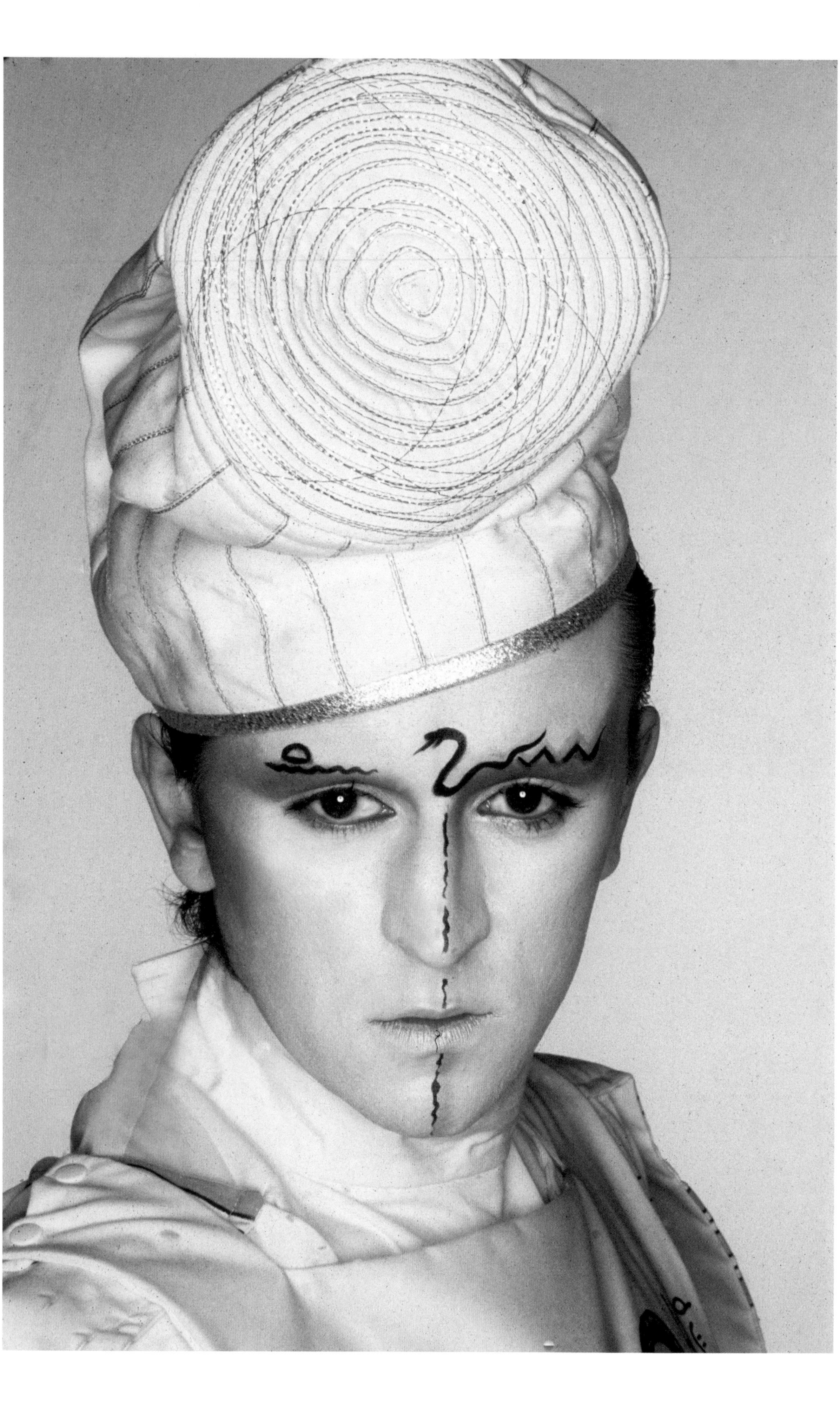

Singer Marilyn wearing *Pervasive Action*, from Stephen Jones's first collection, A/W 1980–81.

Steve Strange wearing a Stephen Jones hat in stitched cotton and lamé, and a tabard by Melissa Caplan. Make-up by Richard Sharah, 1979.

Jones recalls that he 'didn't have a business plan and ... no real workroom':

> 'I just made a collection of hats and I hadn't really thought what would happen when they sold. Just the idea of having a hat shop and an opening party was such a bizarre and wonderful thing that if it had been a failure I would not have minded. But actually, it was a fantastic success! It is so different than today, when people plan their careers – we were just doing it for the Now – that was all that was important. It was all about putting on your blusher – and about how much blusher you could get on!'

The Bavarian-born beauty Gerlinde Costiff/Von Regensburg, a flamboyant fashion personality who sold antique jewellery and handbags from a stall at the Antiquarius Antiques Centre on King's Road, Chelsea, named the hats that Jones created for his boutique. 'That was the thing that changed my attitude to design, the huge catalyst', he remembers:

> 'When I made my first collection of hats there was something missing, but Gerlinde giving them names – like *Monolithic Ego II* and *Functional Dysfunction* – changed the dynamic completely because suddenly they assumed characters. The hats were always very much about the people who were wearing them. If I made a hat for Kim or Julia then that hat was all about them – it was completely reliant on their character. This reflected my training at Lachasse, which was very much about the client, whereas others milliners are very much about the hat.'

Costiff's fashionable socialite friends, Victoria Fernandez and Bianca Juarez, were also among Jones's first paying clients. 'When my phone bill came in Victoria knew she had to buy a hat because otherwise I couldn't pay the phone bill. Without her real support and enthusiasm and drive I would not have managed.'

Jones was also making hats for Susanne Bartsch, who had once worked for Costiff and was now organizing fashion shows bringing London's avant-garde design talents to Tokyo and New York, where she also ran a destination shop. In 1985, Bartsch arranged a midnight showing of Jones's hat collection at Manhattan's Palladium nightclub; attendees included Keith Haring, Dianne Brill and celebrity models Sibylle de St Phalle, Dianne DeWitt and Katoucha. Soon after, Bartsch organized another show in New York that showcased Jones's hats alongside current London design stars David Holah and Stevie Stewart of Bodymap, Dean Bright, and John Richmond and Maria Cornejo. Jones's commercial career really took off when Rhoda Ribner, the influential hat buyer for Bloomingdale's, arrived at his shop in Endell Street and asked to place an order. Jones assumed she might take half a dozen hats but instead she ordered 200;

his wholesale business was launched. He had already begun creating hats for the runway collections of British designers Jasper Conran and Zandra Rhodes, and, meanwhile, commissions from music groups, including Visage, Spandau Ballet, the Thompson Twins, and Annie Lennox, exponentially increased the international exposure of his name and designs. Jones's profile took on an Establishment aspect when Anna Harvey, the *British Vogue* fashion editor advising Diana, Princess of Wales, on her clothes, called to effect an introduction. The hats that Jones designed for the princess were generally 'quite simple and low key, more for her private life than her official duties'.

Although his business and media profile was growing rapidly, Jones's production infrastructure was still homespun. He continued to make all of his hats himself in an improvised workroom in a Warren Street squat – residency there became something of a rite of passage for London's nightclub denizens; Boy George, Marilyn and Kim Bowen all lived there at various times. Bowen and Lee Sheldrick left college to work in Jones's Endell Street shop, which 'really started to be the centre of London nightlife – with Julia and Steve Strange upstairs and Kim and Lee downstairs, it absolutely was party central'. By night, the Endell Street style mongers set the fashion seal on a slew of new nightclubs, as Blitz ceded to Club for Heroes, the Sterling Club, Le Beat Route, Hell and the St Moritz. 'Fashion was very much about the clubs and the music too', Jones remembers. 'It was a British thing – and not just in London. In Liverpool, Bristol, Newcastle, the same sort of thing was going on. *The Face*, *i-D* and *Blitz* magazines were so important, reflecting the fact that like-minded people all over the country were doing their own thing.'

A new chapter in Jones's career opened when his old friend Boy George – a teenage habitué of Blitz – asked him to appear in the video for Culture Club's single 'Do You Really Want to Hurt Me'. Jones styled himself in a pale blue zoot suit from Flip and a red velvet fez of his own design. 'I looked like a character in 1946 at the Café de Paris in Tangier', he recalls. Jean Paul Gaultier saw the video and asked Jones to appear in his first menswear show, which had been inspired by that *Pépé le Moko* vision. Philippe Krootchey, the singer and DJ, did the music for the show and through him Jones met a group of Parisian society fashionistas, including Sibylle de St Phalle who came to London to work for him. 'She was so glamorous', Jones remembers, 'with that whole notion of French coquetry being passed down from mother to daughter'. St Phalle was also well connected and introduced Jones to Azzedine Alaïa: 'He'd just left Thierry Mugler and he wasn't showing collections so he said to me "I don't need hats because I don't do shows but I know somebody who does".' The result was an introduction to Thierry Mugler. Around the same

Bottom: Stephen Jones in his workroom in the Warren Street squat, making a leather cap with barbed wire. Picture appeared in *So-en* magazine, May 1981.

Right: Stephen Jones and Sibylle de St Phalle, Jones's first PR-assistant, 1984. She later on became John Galliano's first PR-assistant.

Zandra Rhodes wearing a Stephen Jones hat. She was Jones' first designer client in A/W 1982–83. Make-up by Richard Sharah.

Jasper Conran advertisement, featuring a Stephen Jones hat in perforated felt. British *Vogue* 1986.

time, Gaultier asked Jones if he would create the hats for his womenswear show, inspired, like the menswear show, by a 1940s vision of Morocco. And so began Jones's life on fashion's international stage.

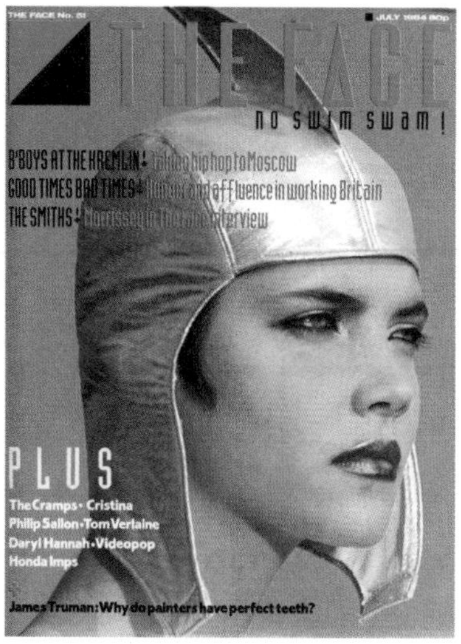

Top: *The Face* cover, featuring a silver balaclava by Stephen Jones, July 1986.

Bottom: Stephen Jones, Sibylle de St Phalle and Jean Paul Gaultier at Albert de Paname's *Fête des Chapeaux de Stephen Jones* at Le Palace, Paris, March 1985. Sibylle wears a headdress composed of a picture of Lucille Ball's eyes and mouth.

Right: Boy George wearing a Stephen Jones hat made by Bouke De Vries, 1983.

LILY ALLEN

I meet Lily Allen at the end of a day of interviews at The Ivy club in early December. This is practically home territory for the singer, a new part of the London media habitat she grew up in and that she now securely occupies in her own right. She is promoting her second album, *It's Not Me, It's You*, and by the looks of it there is no more appropriate name to subtitle the interview that is winding down at the moment. The singer looks thoroughly agitated and as the interview ends she makes

Text Jo-Ann Furniss

Lily Allen wearing *Louvre*, S/S 2009, by Stephen Jones in *Love* magazine issue 1, 2008.

Pink wearing *Fiona*, a Stephen Jones painted leather cap with barbed wire and metal mesh. A/W 2003–04.

STEPHEN JONES, THE ACCENT OF FASHION

Anna Piaggi
Journalist, Italian *Vogue*
Fashion Contributor

Photography
Bardo Fabiani

Art Direction
Luca Stoppini

Studio Direction
Lesley Robeson

Hair & Make-up
Maurizio Massari

Set Design
Bruno Bambara

Coordination
Moreno Fardin

Pages 96–105

Stephen Jones & Anna Piaggi, with Luca Stoppini & Bardo Fabiani
Special commission, Milan, 2010.

SYRINX
CIAGA

Autumn Winter
2000 - 2001

many
many jewels
made in
Italy

FASHION ALGEBRA

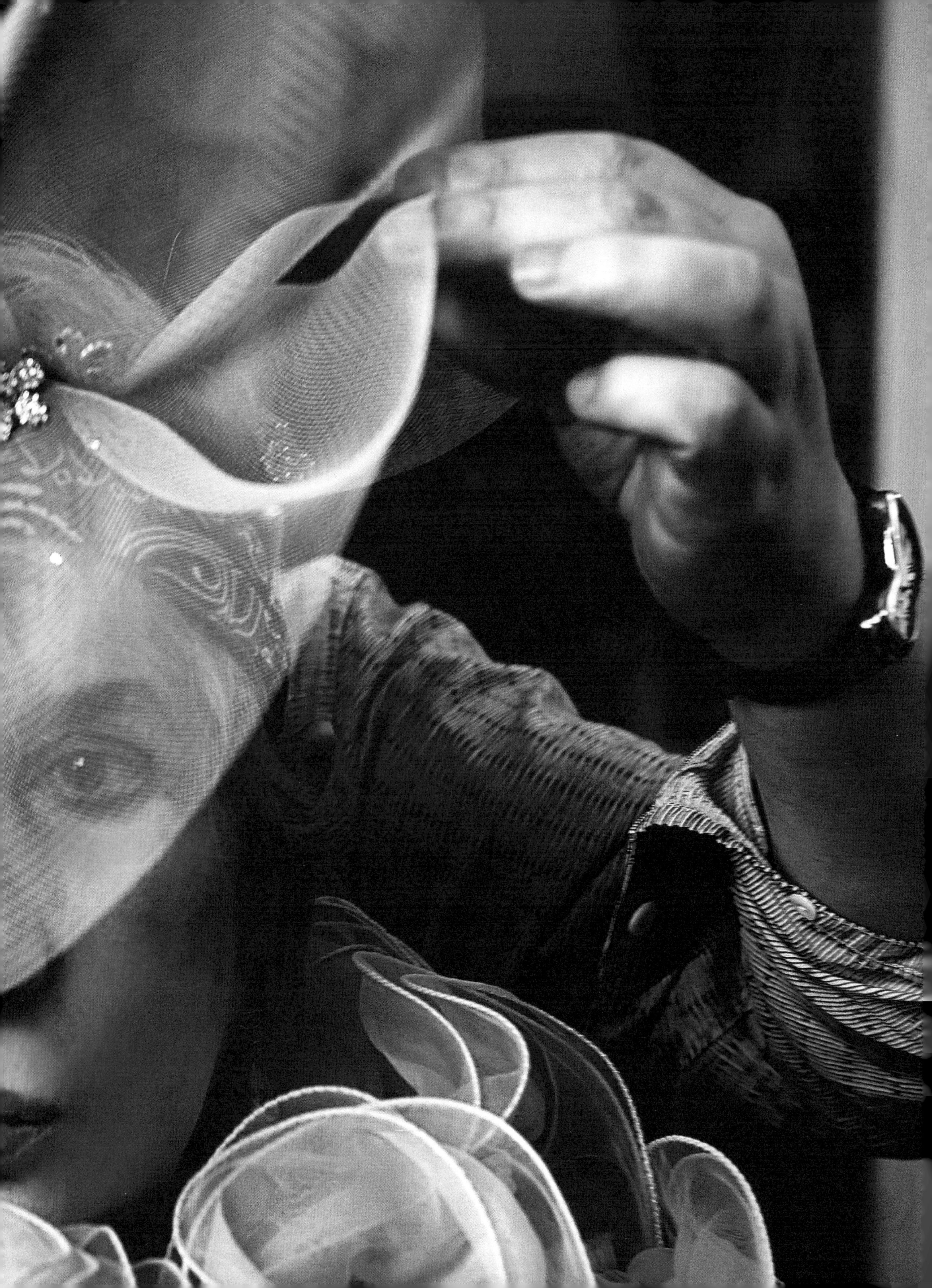

Andy Warhol

Rose Venus
HNL

Alt. 2472 m.

Frivolity

HANA

STEPHEN JONES & HIS COLLABORATIONS

Suzy Menkes
Fashion journalist at the
International Herald Tribune

Picture the moment in the run-up to a Christian Dior haute couture show. John Galliano is working silently in the Paris studio with friend and ally, the master milliner Stephen Jones. The designer is looking at the arc of a silhouette, the drape of a skirt and the tilt of a hat. 'I often work through a mirror for most of my decisions and I always see Stephen's reflection,' says Galliano. 'He is reading my every nuance. He is studying my face. I don't need to say anything — he can read my mind. We are definitely on the same page at the same time — before anyone opens his mouth', he continues. 'At that point there is not much talking. It's a magical moment. It's eye contact. We're like a silent movie.' In this rare glimpse into the artistic collaboration between two hyper-creative people, one begins to understand the symbiotic relationship shared by Jones and Galliano.

Jones's partnerships with cutting-edge designers are central to his career — and often to the development of the designers themselves. A list of his collaborations reads like a history of 20th- and 21st-century fashion. There was work with 1980s fashion icon Claude Montana; the iconic *Harris Tweed* crown for Vivienne Westwood in 1987; a long-standing relationship with Rei Kawakubo of Comme des Garçons; hats made from human hair for Josephus Thimister's 1994 collection; and more recently collaborations with Marc Jacobs, L'Wren Scott, Basso & Brooke, Walter Van Beirendonck and Giles Deacon.

'It was such an opportunity to work with Stephen — he is such a fount of knowledge', says Deacon, who started working with Jones in 2006. 'I almost don't like to call it millinery — the things we have done are not like the concept of normal hats', he continues. 'And I love the appeal of the hats, each season as a complement to the collection. They're not just decorative, but an integral part.'

His words sum up the experience of all the designers who work with Jones and apply particularly to Galliano, a fashion ally and friend since the two first met at London's Blitz club in the 1980s. That was when Jones hung out with Boy George and the band Spandau Ballet, and Galliano claims that the snazzily-dressed 'mad hatter' declined to make hats for the new graduate from Saint Martin's School of Art.

Stephen Jones & Mondino
Toile in calico of a Christian Dior Haute Couture dress and a Stephen Jones hat from cardboard and paper, both for Christian Dior Haute Couture, S/S 2005. Archives Jean-Baptiste Mondino, published in *The New York Times*, early 2005.

'He looked at me and said: "I don't think so, dear!"' recalls Galliano, who has now been working with Jones for nearly 20 years.

Their collaboration started at John Galliano and continued at Givenchy, after Bernard Arnault, chairman of luxury group LVMH, made the designer creative director of the Paris house. This shake-up of the classic label was ultimately short-lived but Jones remembers the *Winter Ascot* collection as a forest of a runway with 'girls sitting on a bed and all the things John loved: bias-cut dresses in red to pink – the collection was very lyrical, each outfit told a story'. One legacy of that collaboration was the pink heart-shaped hat that Madonna wore to the world premiere of *Evita* in 1996.

Galliano's time at Givenchy proved a rehearsal for his transformation of Christian Dior from bourgeois and lady-like to dramatic and dynamic. Ever since his first 17-piece wisp of an all-black collection promenaded through strewn roses and around a fallen chandelier, the Paris fashion audiences have been captivated.

Top: Madonna wearing a Stephen Jones for Givenchy hat at the première of *Evita*, Los Angeles, 1996.

Bottom: Stephen Jones for Thierry Mugler, A/W 1986–87. Halo in pleated gold lame; the dress was made on model Iman, Thierry Mugler stapling the gold lame on the velour dress just before she made her entrance.

Right: Stephen Jones for Thierry Mugler, A/W 1986.

Galliano had been studying the sophistication of Parisian haute couture, and his move to Dior confirmed how he has come to develop his collections: a long, thoughtful period when he creates his 'bible' – the book of references that builds up a story line – followed by the creation of the garments themselves. 'There was a huge amount of preparation – John's research and analysis were meticulous and the clothes were the process', says Jones about how the shows came together. 'And John was very personally involved. From the beginning he thought about hats. Everything was designed in tandem. Almost every designer thinks of the silhouette. John thought about the whole woman. It is very unusual and maybe why his shows have such a unique place.'

Collections follow a similar creation process even now; Jones translates Galliano's ideas and his own research into multiple sketches divided into such categories as silhouettes, textures and fabrics. By this point, the milliner will have 'gone to several fittings, taken notes and got involved in character', says Galliano, and, from that base, he helps to define how the 'figure' at the centre of the show evolves, 'amending colours, fabric and feelings to make her who she is'. Drawings are presented to the Dior team, with around 20 designs being made into *toiles* (canvas patterns). Artisans then sculpt the wooden blocks on to which the fabrics are moulded or construct wire filigree shapes to form a delicate tracery. Imaginative trimmings are added to the hats, which, finally, as with any live performance, take part in a dress rehearsal before being approved and sent down the catwalk.

Pour plisser au soleil, une robe du soir en jersey de cachemire et incrustée de coquille Saint Jacques en laine or. La parure est de Jones (Stephen).

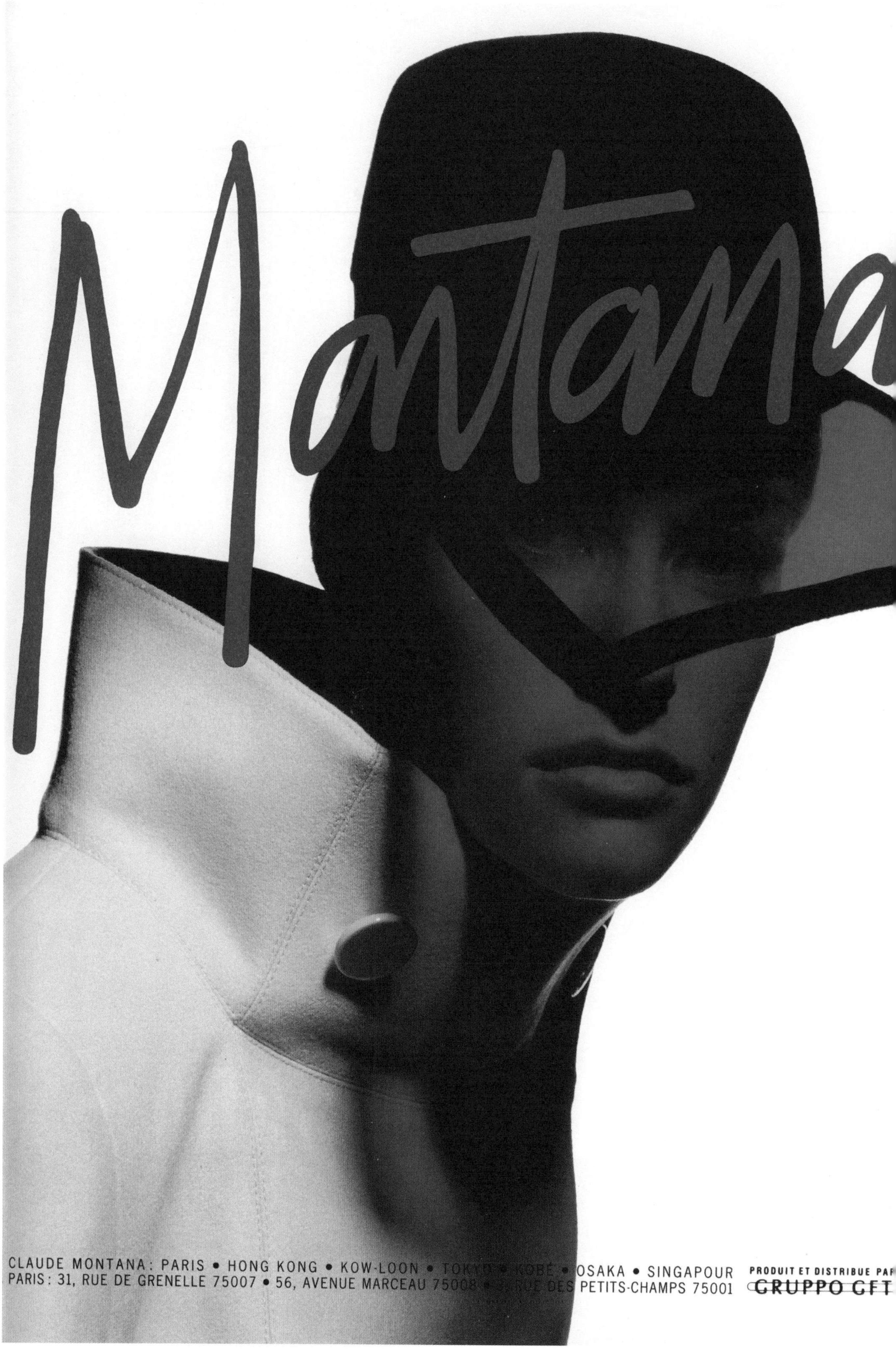

Stephen Jones for Claude Montana, advertisement in *Vogue* Paris N°718, August 1991.

BUCOL
LANVIN
PARIS

Typically, a Galliano figure is taken from the past and deeply researched. In 1998, Giovanni Boldini's portrait of the Marchesa Luisa Casati sparked Galliano to create his Dior spring–summer couture collection around her. The Marchesa was a famous and exotic figure in European society in the first three decades of the twentieth century. Muse and inspiration to many artists, she commissioned them to paint her and insure her visual immortality. For his collection, Galliano gave the models Casati's extravagantly fashionable look, topping off long, sinuous gowns with fountainous black feather hats spilling over with white lace.

Jones worked with Galliano on those first collections when Amanda Harlech (the elegant muse who later went to work with Karl Lagerfeld at Chanel) stimulated the young fashion designer's fantasy and poetic vision. The milliner showed his team spirit by acting as accessory maker and dresser, helping the models into their crinolines and placing each hat. He still reserves this last task for himself, notes Galliano — 'He knows whether a hat needs to look blown away. He knows the tilt of the hat on every single girl's face and [her] morphology. He is an engineer.'

Top: Stephen Jones for Lanvin, S/S 1991 Headdress made from gelatined chiffon.

Bottom: Stephen Jones's first hat, made as an intern at Lachasse to show Shirley Hex, head of the millinery workroom 1977.

Left: Stephen Jones for Lanvin, S/S 1991 Metal beads and rhinestones on a hair net.

It is Jones's placement of each hat that defines it; a decorative circle landing like a flying saucer on one ear over a floating, romantic dress; the rakish tilt of a silken black riding hat evoking the aristocratic world of fox hunting. This last hat belonged to an animalistic collection shown in Versailles' Orangerie in 1999. Galliano recalls trying to deconstruct 'hunting, shooting and fishing' and creating 'hunting clothes and ball dresses with an aristocratic feel'; Jones remembers the unbridled energy of those furry pieces and the fact that he got 'into huge trouble from an ethical point of view'. The *Madame Butterfly* show of January 2007 was another occasion of complete symbiosis between hatter and designer, resulting in exquisite Japanese-inspired haute couture and memorable headwear, including pagoda hats, chopstick wigs, cherry blossom branches and miniature lanterns. Jones studied the research book to create original textures with absolute authenticity. Sometimes hats had to be improvised or put together at literally the eleventh hour; Jones was still concocting a red folded-blanket hat minutes before it appeared on stage at Galliano's autumn-winter 2002–03 show.

It was this spirit of improvisation that had landed Jones his first millinery opportunity interning at the London couture house, Lachasse, in 1976. Taking a plastic flower that his mother had received from a petrol station, the 19-year-old Saint Martin's student sprayed it silver and used it to decorate a quickly-constructed pillbox hat.

Even today — especially for the John Galliano collections — it seems that any material, however unlikely, can be put to use. Take, for example, *Fishbone*, a skeletal form paired with a graphic dress for autumn–winter 1999–91, or *Mouth-watering*, a thunderbird hat made from wooden lollipop sticks in 1996. Galliano has to ask; 'Is there anything that is not pliable in his hands? He has a lightness of touch, but the materials are toughened and soaked in traditional ways. I don't think that [to] anything I asked him to do, he ever said "no".' The designer stresses the importance of Jones to his career; 'I can't remember when Stephen wasn't part of the family' — referring to a tight-knit, mostly British, clan that includes master-cutter Bill Gaytten, DJ Jeremy Healy, and Steven Robinson, his right hand and realizer of dreams until he died in 2007.

Naturally, Galliano asked Jones to create hats for his personal wardrobe too, since he wears them not just to take a bow on the runway but every day of his life. The designer recalls his demands for headgear: a bandana, sun-bleached and dyed with just the right degree of *degradé* (shading); or a *Gavroche* beret, inspired by illustrations of the fictional character from Victor Hugo's epic 19th-century novel *Les Misérables*.

Oriole Cullen, co-curator with Jones of *Hats: An Anthology by Stephen Jones*, an exhibition held at the Victoria and Albert Museum, London, in 2009, is well acquainted with the milliner's unusual materials and techniques. 'Apart from intricate sewing skills, [his] team is expert at manipulating Perspex, dyeing fabrics, spray painting and a range of skills which one would never automatically associate with hats', she says. 'It's interesting to watch Stephen working with designers', she continues. 'He tries different shapes on the model's head and talks through changes and adaptations. It is essentially the equivalent of the couturier draping on a mannequin.'

The materials that Jones uses for his hats are available for all his shows, but his methods vary depending on which designer he is working with. That variety is epitomized by contrasting Comme des Garçons with Dior – 'Chalk and cheese!' Jones proclaims, when asked to describe the enormous differences between working with Rei Kawakubo and John Galliano. And it is easy to understand why he uses that traditional English expression for polar opposites.

Meeting by chance in an airport three decades ago, the milliner and the Tokyo-based designer began working together in a world 'inconceivable to people today', Jones recalls; there was no computer, no cell-phone images; no PDFs. The collaboration even goes back to the years before fax machines became wide-spread (mid-1980s). Each single sketch had to be sent by mail and would take five days to clear Japanese customs.

Stephen Jones for John Galliano
Fishbone, a skate skeleton made from paper straws, A/W 1999–2000.
MoMu Collection B02/6
Published in *The New Yorker*, September 20, 1999, page 103.

Stephen Jones for John Galliano
Mouth-watering, Native American thunderbird made from lollipop sticks, A/W 1996–97.

Stephen Jones for John Galliano. Bathing beauty hat, made by Julia Wigley from Nagoire feathers, tulle and taffeta, S/S 2009.

Paris 16th Nov '95 -

Dearest Stephen,

Pure magic, made in Heaven, blown together as if by God, you are a genius.

John Galliano

Ecole de Danse

JOHN GALLIANO SHOWROOM : PASSAGE DU CHEVAL BLANC - COUR DE MAI
2, RUE DE LA ROQUETTE - 75011 PARIS - TEL : 33 (1) 47 00 29 51 - FAX : 33 (1) 47 00 93 55

I Take my Hat off To You Mr. Jones!

JP Gaultier

Dear Stephen

I love the Dover Street Market exhibition. It is really great – witty, powerful & creative.

Best love for 2005

Suzy

x

Anna Piaggi

Milano, 24th July 2003

Dear Stephen,
here the polaroids of the hat you gave me in Paris, which I arranged "à la gipsy" ....
are by Roberto,
maker and

give them to
Love Anna

Clockwise from top left: Thankyou notes from John Galliano, Jean Paul Gaultier, Anna Piaggi & Suzy Menkes.

Stephen Jones for Christian Dior Haute Couture
Christian Dior Haute Couture anniversary show at Versailles, A/W 2007–08. Decor by Michael Howells.

Left: *Viviane Orth inspirée par Manet*
Rococo boater in Swiss straw, stitched by Cheri Bibi.

Right: *Olga Sherer inspirée par Gruau*
Palette coolie with paintbrush, made by Veroliv.

Top: Stephen Jones for John Galliano, A/W 2004–05
Wigs, turbans, hats, hair decorations and jewellery.

Right: Stephen Jones for John Galliano, S/S 1997
Charming, mini coolie hats in coins, silver lace and charms.
MoMu Collection B02/25

Lava, S/S 2003

Stephen Jones for Christian Dior Haute Couture, S/S 2004
Model Erin O'Connor as Tutunkhamun.
Illustration by David Downton.

If Jones asked the cerebral Kawakubo for a brief, the reply came: 'There is no brief'. So the earliest work for a Comme des Garçons summer collection was what Jones calls 'rough and ready', meaning different styles of straw hats, turbans with raffia wrapped round and caps made out of mesh. When the fax became their new communication tool, the duo 'spoke' in a terse fashion language. 'Rei would say "something very summery" — and then it would be word association', says Jones — '"Summer." "Straw?" "Dark." "Black straw?" "Black straw with holes in it!"'

Adrian Joffe, Kawakubo's partner in life and business, acts as a conduit between Tokyo and the Stephen Jones studio in Covent Garden, London. He describes the process that he has observed and shared:

'With Rei, when she works with a fellow creator, there is never a sitting down and brainstorming, no samples to-ing and fro-ing, no back and forth, no exchange of ideas. There is a first meeting (and sometimes not even) when the lines are drawn about who does what. Usually it is Rei who does everything and they approve it! It can only work with trust and respect. Rei will do everything, or she will let the other person do everything, within the decided parameters. With Stephen, it is the same, although the level of respect is very deep and the trust is entire.'

One memorable collection for Joffe was *Lost Empire*, the spring–summer 2006 collection, in which Kawakubo created an elegiac ode to Jones's home country: Great Britain and its fading royal heritage. 'She just told him "CROWNS" — and Stephen had total freedom to create at will. Rei chose to use 80 per cent of what he made', Joffe notes. 'More recently, she sent a photo of an old schoolgirl hat and said "straw and poplin". Stephen then went away and made six beautiful, fresh schoolgirl hats in straw and poplin.'

Although Jones does not work every season with Comme des Garçons — only when it seems appropriate to the designer — there is a close bond between them. Kawakubo is in no doubt of the active creative role that he has played in her work. 'It has only been possible to continue to work with Stephen, on and off for the past 30 years, because he shares my belief that without creation there can be no progress', she says. 'And he works with all his heart and mind. That is all I ever ask for.' In 2005, Kawakubo and Joffe invited Jones to set-up shop in Dover Street Market for his 25 year retrospective exhibition, giving the milliner total freedom to do as he pleased. Kawakubo came especially to London for the opening.

Stephen Jones for Comme des Garçons, A/W 2006–07
Tulle beret and mask with marguerites, French *Vogue*, Autumn 2006.

The close collaboration that Jones shares with Kawakubo is in stark contrast to how the milliner works with Marc Jacobs, who presents him with a completed image. Jones embraces this process too:

'Marc has an encyclopedic knowledge of film and a fantastic memory of the line of a hat in a Julie Christie movie or the angle of a beret from Saint Laurent in the 1970s. Or it will be Roman ladies going shopping in 1967 [wearing] Valentino. It has to be the perfect silhouette but to look contemporary. Marc's unique thing is to be able to take fashion from the past, put a zip up the back and make it modern.'

Stephen Jones for Comme des Garçons,
A/W 2006–07
Felt beret.

The first of his long-lasting fashion partnerships, Jones's collaboration with 1980s fashion hero Claude Montana spanned 15 years. He uses the term 'exigence' — meaning the exacting demand for excellence — to define the essence of Montana's style. The designer applied his high standards to architectural lines and subtle shades of colour; to a streamlined look topped off with a head moulded by a balaclava helmet. 'Working with Montana was an extraordinary training — I learnt about line, tailoring, silhouette and restraint', says Jones, who started with Galliano when the collaboration with Montana ended.

As well as designers, throughout his career Jones has always worked with less visible, but highly important, hand workers. In the fashion show equation, they are the *modelistes* — the individuals who actually handcraft the hats. In fact, it is often the London-based workers who do the lion's share — Galliano's first show for Givenchy was nearly ruined by the 35-hour working week in France; the *modelistes* were obliged to leave on Friday afternoon instead of carrying on through the weekend for Monday's runway presentation. Regardless of which side of the Channel they are originate, Curator Oriole Cullen is adamant that all of Jones's hats for Christian Dior have couture status 'as they are all made completely by hand in either the Covent Garden workshop or in the Dior atelier'.

Giles Deacon is the most recent designer to persuade Jones to work with him and he appreciates it, knowing that it is a badge of honour for the milliner to agree to work with him:

'I love to work with Stephen and his relevance now is as strong as it has ever been. He has a wealth of experience and will be able to pinpoint a piece of embroidery from 1937. I am so often surprised by him when he comes up with certain things, like metal rods of wire for the porcelain collection (the autumn–winter collection 2010 was shown in the Italian porcelain factory Richard Ginori). The time spent — and the effect included with it — is all pretty phenomenal.'

Stephen Jones for Comme des Garçons,
S/S 2006
Crown made from Meccano.

Deacon recalls how he sat in the hatter's studio, while Lesley Robeson,

Stephen Jones for Christian Dior Haute Couture, A/W 2005–06. Hat inspired by a Catholic crown.

Josiane Le Magueresse and Maria Bazzini working on the first Christian Dior Haute Couture collection in the Atelier Mode at Dior, 1997. Josiane was the premier at the renowned wartime milliner Paulette, Paris.

Stephen Jones for Christian Dior Haute Couture, A/W 1999–2000
Backstage at the Orangerie, Versailles, 1999.

Right: *Lupina*, A/W 2006–07
MoMu Collection B08/21

Stephen Jones for Antonio Berardi
Top left: S/S 2005; Top right: A/W 2005–06.

Right: Stephen Jones for Marc Jacobs
Hat made from an image of Maria Callas as Medea, Dallas, 1958.
Embroidery by Soidera from ultra fine Japanese bugle beads.
Published in French *Vogue,* March 2008.

Jones's assistant for 21 years, typed at the computer, and showed Jones *Pac-Man* games on his phone screen. 'I thought the visuals were really interesting', says Deacon. Inspired by the iconic 1980s arcade game, he went on to work a science-fiction theme into his spring–summer 2009 show with Jones creating giant, shiny helmets that curved over the models' heads in a space-age arc. 'He has quite a cartoon sensibility for his hats, because [his] clothes are quite serious and architectural', comments Jones. 'Giles is such a charmer and we always have a wonderful time.'

The appreciation is mutual: 'I love the formality of the small studio in Great Queen Street, with the delicate mauve and the beautiful hat stands. He is super, super good, we are making something beautiful and I like working with him because it is really, really good fun.'

Multi-coloured Butterfly of Love, S/S 1993
Multi-coloured tulle.

Right: Stephen Jones for Claude Montana, S/S 1987
Bridal veil in iridescent lamé. Appeared in *Collezioni*.

Stephen Jones for Giles Deacon, S/S 2009, published in *PLASTIQUE* magazine. Resin hat inspired by the 1980s computer game *Pac-Man*, made by Stephen Diaper.

Top: Stephen Jones for Hussein Chalayan, S/S 2007

Left: Stephen Jones for Dirk Van Saene, S/S 2001
Wig made from ostrich feathers.

Stephen Jones for Walter Van Beirendonck
Top left: Hat made from wood and wool, *Skin King* collection A/W 2008–09.
Top right: Hat made from papier-mâché, *Sex Clown* collection S/S 2008.

Right: Stephen Jones for Walter Van Beirendonck, A/W 2010–11
Plastic wig and giant felt top hat.

Stephen Jones for Walter Van Beirendonck, *Avatar* collection, A/W 1997–98. Plastic hat in the shape of a computer.

Stephen Jones for Walter Van Beirendonck, *Avatar* collection, A/W 1997–98. Hat with feather and metal frame with red perspex, casting 'make-up' on the model's face (frame made by Inge Grognard).

STEPHEN JONES & BRITISHNESS

Oriole Cullen
Curator of Modern Textiles and Fashion at the Victoria and Albert Museum, London

Throughout his career, the theme of Britishness has been a keystone of Stephen Jones's design aesthetic. While fellow designers Vivienne Westwood and John Galliano frequently reference notions of Britain in their work, Jones's particular brand of Britishness adopts a slightly skewed and frequently humorous vision. As Rebecca Arnold notes, for Westwood it is 'aristocracy and empire, not suburbia and parochialism that inspires her'.[1] Yet for Jones, who designed Westwood's famous *Harris Tweed* crown of 1987, and whose spring–summer 1988 collection was entitled *Sunset on Suburbia*, it is *all* of these things blended together that for him signify Britain. Indeed Andrew Bolton's definition of Britishness – a term that 'embraces the diverse, disparate and diasporic character of the country (or rather countries)' – is exemplified in the variety and inclusiveness of Jones's body of work.[2]

National identity is an evolving and invented construct and, as such, there will always be motifs that encapsulate the essence of a particular country or state. In sartorial matters, British dress can be summed up in the words – tweeds, tartans, tailoring and tiaras. These elements have all figured in Jones's work as vital indicators of an all-encompassing and affectionate vision of the idiosyncrasies of British life. His *Millinery Computer* collection of autumn–winter 1998–99 offered a selection of hats catering to different activities, with hats entitled *Charity Lunch*, *Christening*, *Launching a Ship* and *Seduction* mixed in with *Walking the Dogs*, *School Run* and *Neighbourhood Watch*. Like photographer Martin Parr, Jones finds charm and distinction in mundane objects and the instances of everyday life. Accordingly, his output has included hats named *Tupperware*, *Vimto* and *Andrex*.

The singularly British top hat has featured in Stephen Jones collections since 1983, and the milliner has become known for his playful miniature versions of this iconic hat. As an article of men's formal dress, today the traditional top hat is rarely worn except at Royal Ascot, formal weddings or royal events. Many contemporary wearers tend to sport top hats that have been handed down through families, rather than new versions

1. Arnold, Rebecca, 'Vivienne Westwood's Anglomania' in *The Englishness of English Dress*, Eds. Christopher Breward, Becky Conekin and Caroline Cox (Oxford and New York, 2002), p.161

2. Bolton, Andrew, *AngloMania: Tradition and Transgression in British Fashion* (New York, 2006), p.13

Stephen Jones & David Bailey
Special commission, London, 2010.

THE HOLIDAY ISSUE
i-D MAGAZINE NO.50 AUGUST 1987 £1.50 / $4.50
i-D
"trendy fashion magazine"
50
ANNIVERSARY
SPECIAL
GLOBAL LONDON
WORLDWIDE FASHION
KINGS! QUEENS!!
AND COMMONERS!!
5 013071 000294
VIVIENNE WESTWOOD
CROWNS HER PRINCESS

Top: The Pet Shop Boys, with a Union Jack felt bowler hat by Stephen Jones.

Left: *i-D* magazine cover, August 1987. Featuring Harris tweed crown by Stephen Jones for Vivienne Westwood, A/W 1987–88.

fitted for them personally. Likewise, when Jones attends special occasions, he does not wear a product of his atelier but his grandfather's top hat, a handed-down object in the great British tradition; he explains, 'My father's top hat doesn't fit me at all but my grandfather and I have the exact same shaped head!'[3]

Jones makes many overt references to Britain in his collections – he has fondly manipulated the Union Jack into a series of dramatic hats, including a felt bowler in 2000, now in the Museum of London's collections, and his *Anna P* top hat of 2009. He also works more subtle Britishness into his work, as found in his witty appropriation and translation of ideas into visual puns with a particularly British sense of humour. Michael Carter has referred to hats as 'little theatres of ornament',[4] and certainly when Stephen Jones hats are involved there is always a little story or drama being played out upon the wearer's head.

Within the norms of accepted and traditional dress codes, the hat can become an agent that breaks conventional rules and restrictions, offering liberation, exaggeration and drama; in a sense, the hat becomes a sartorial embodiment of Mikhail Bakhtin's theory of the carnivalesque. Jones has always acknowledged the importance of *whimsy* within his work. When invited to be guest editor of *.Cent* magazine in 2006, he chose *whimsy* – an odd or fanciful idea; light fanciful humour; a whim – as the theme for his edition. He is particularly inspired by a number of 20th-century British artists and photographers, including Rex Whistler, Cecil Beaton and Angus McBean, who all took a singularly ludic approach to their work. Prominent artists during the 1930s, these individuals saw the comic potential of surrealism and imbued their work with a mixture of theatricality and strangeness, qualities inherent in Jones's hat designs. Jones also points to the book *Austerity/Binge: Decorative Arts of the Forties and Fifties* by Bevis Hillier as an important influence on the development of his own design aesthetic.[5] He believes that 'in the world of hats *whimsy* is crucial. Lightness of touch, spontaneity, frivolity spiced with a touch of the bizarre give the wearer the unique visual and emotional boost that only a hat can bring'.[6]

1980 was an unusual time for a young St Martin's graduate to launch a career in millinery. While the anarchic style of punk remained visibly present in every town in Britain, Jones (himself a former punk) was entering the realms of a profession that typified notions of respectability and which was heavily identified with the rules and etiquette of the Establishment. While punk was the universal style reference for British teenagers in the late 1970s, hats nonetheless remained a staple of their mothers' wardrobes, brought out for special occasions, including weddings,

3. Stephen Jones interview with Oriole Cullen (16.02.2010)

4. Carter, Michael, *Putting a Face on Things: Studies in Imaginary Materials* (Sydney, 1996), p.116

5. Hillier, Bevis, *Austerity/Binge: Decorative Arts of the Forties and Fifties* (London, 1975)

6. Jones, Stephen, ed., *.Cent* magazine (autumn–winter 2006), p.5

A shining

NEW SEASON

for British evenings

Night moves with a difference and the loud sophistication of gleaming brocade and panne velvet. Catch the glamour of the new ornamentation, sculpted to fit in clinging bodices and delicious mixes of satins and sequins. Skirts blossom in witty ruffles or rise to the occasion and sit decisively above the knee. Just add one mad little hat and serve on the rocks... diamonds or sapphires will do

Top: Naomi Campbell in *Elle* UK, in one of her first ever modelling assignments, wearing *Uplifting*, A/W 1988–89.

Left: Stephen Jones for Comme des Garçons, A/W 2007–08
Published in *Popeye* magazine, August 2007.

christenings and funerals. Internationally, by the 1960s the hat had reached the end of its run as a key part of every woman's wardrobe. Its fashionability had been swept away in the onset of youth fashions that sought distance from the codes and connotations of the previous generation. Hairstyles, not hats, were now the fashion focus for the head. The advent of central heating and increased accessibility to cars meant the hat also lost the practicality that had previously made it an essential accessory. In 1971, fashion writer Kennedy Fraser observed, 'As a social object the hat has ceased to be; as a decorative accessory it long ago ceased to evolve'.[7] By the late 1970s, in high fashion circles where the visual impact of a hat was widely acknowledged, only Karl Lagerfeld at Chloé was regularly sending hats onto the catwalk.[8] Despite this absence, in Britain the hat retained a place in occasionwear and the formal wardrobe.

The survival of the hat in Britain can be attributed to a number of factors. The British love of 'dressing up' is well known and, as Ian Buruma has observed, there is a great appreciation of the sartorial 'freedom to be something one is not'.[9] An understanding of the transformative power of dress cuts across both age and class divides. That inclination to dress for the occasion is instantly visible on any Saturday night across the British Isles, from coatless teenagers in sequinned mini-dresses to smartly attired theatre goers, dinner party attendees and those heading to a local bar or restaurant; nearly all will have made an effort to change some aspect of their clothing. This shared conviction in 'being properly attired' is especially focussed when a special occasion is in the offing, thus presenting a lifeline for the hat. Jones believes that the English take a unique pride in donning a hat, which equates to the wearing of national costume in other countries: 'In Austria or Sweden, for example, it is customary to wear traditional folk dress for important occasions. The English don't have a national costume as such but they do love to wear a hat to an appropriate occasion.'[10]

While the young Stephen Jones was launching a revolution in the millinery world – with his emphasis on street fashion and the music scene of the New Romantics – the traditional British millinery industry (which he would later join as a major player) continued quietly working away, albeit on a much reduced scale to 50 years earlier. That customer base would later offer the framework for Jones's expansion, allowing for solid seasonal sales beyond the often ephemeral demands of the worlds of music and high fashion. One of the principal factors in the survival of the British millinery trade was the 'Season' and its modern day remnants. Traditionally, the Season occurred during the summer months when the court and society descended upon London to partake in a programme of perennial events in and around the city. It formally began with the

Top: Model Susie Bick, favourite of John Galliano and wife of Nick Cave, wearing a branch of felt holly on the cover of *Harpers & Queen*, December 1990.

Below: Linda Evangelista wearing *Quintess*, S/S 1988, on the invitation for the opening of the exhibition *Mad Hatters* at the Australian National Gallery, August–December 1992.

Right: Photographer Gitte Meldgaard, modelling *Bali-Higher*, S/S 1993, inspired by Madame Yevonde's *Goddess* series.

7. Fraser, Kennedy, *The Fashionable Mind: Reflections on Fashion 1970–1981* (New York, 1981), p.56

8. Stephen Jones interview with Oriole Cullen (18.05.2010)

9. Buruma, Ian, 'Tell a Man by His Clothes' in *AngloMania*, p.17

10. Stephen Jones interview with Oriole Cullen (18.05.2010)

Drawing of *Anemone Fantasia* by
fashion illustrator Barbara Hulanicki.

Top: Advertisement for the Ascot Races, 16–19 June 2009, featuring *Anemone Fantasia*, inspired by Stephen Jones's research at the V&A Museum for the exhibition *Hats. An Anthology by Stephen Jones*. Particular inspiration was drawn by the hat *Langoustine Fantasia* by 1960s milliner Simone Mirman.

Left: *Gazebo*, A/W 1994–95
Garden scene hat inspired by the romantic theatre sets of Oliver Messel. Made from straw, chenille, flock, cotton, acetate.

Soirée Scarabée, S/S 1993, inspired by boyhood canoe trips in the backwaters of the Thames.

Designer & Art Director Simon Costin dressed as the 'Green Man' outside his Museum of British Folklore. Top hat in painted leather by Lesley Robeson with shelving and *objets trouvés*.

Top: Suzy Menkes wears *Hong Kong*, S/S 2006, made by Véronique Tissières. Photographed when receiving her Order of the British Empire with the Yeoman Warders of the Tower of London.

Left: *Regatta*, S/S 1999
Trompe l'oeil boater, nicknamed *Titanic* by the model workroom.
MoMu Collection B02/7

opening of the Summer Exhibition at the Royal Academy of Arts, followed by the RHS Chelsea Flower Show, Ascot, the Henley Regatta and the Wimbledon Championship, amongst other events, finally closing with horse racing at Goodwood. In 1999, Jones's *Pic'n'mix* collection paid tribute to the Season with *Ladies Day* (a hat made of white feathers in the shape of a bird's wing), *Chelsea* (a silk beret) and *Centre Court* (a boater of green straw, denoting the famous Wimbledon grass tennis court with a tiny white ball suspended above it).

Although the Season is often identified with the wealthier sections of society, events such as Ascot and Henley have traditionally been open to all comers. Ladies Day at Ascot has always attracted women from a wide and varied demographic who compete to be the one wearing the most dramatic hat. From the 1960s onwards, the annual appearance of Mrs Gertrude Shilling (mother of milliner David Shilling) in theatrical and often gigantic hats was eagerly anticipated and each year became a nationally reported phenomenon. The Royal Enclosure may be set aside for royalty and other special guests, but social mobility within the British class system ensures a constant flow of new blood and aspirational fervour that helps avoid stagnation at this popular event in the British calendar. Fresh attendees to Ascot embrace the dress code, which requires that a hat be worn, more than happy to be assimilated into the group. Buruma observes of English dress: 'The importance of posing, of cutting a dash, through outrage as well as originality, is part of the strong but porous class system'.[11]

The most significant reason for the survival of the Season's traditional dress codes has been the royal family. The long reign of Queen Elizabeth II has afforded Britain a familiar and imposing head of state, whose classic style of dress has altered little during her time on the throne and, crucially, includes a hat. The Queen's wardrobe is carefully constructed based on the demands of her job. The need to be visible in a crowd means that she chooses distinctive colours; her hems must be weighted to avoid any situation where strong gusts of wind might whip at her skirt; she must be able to remove or add a layer swiftly, adjusting to changes in temperature when moving from indoor events to outdoor appearances; and her clothes must always be accessible via uncomplicated fastenings in order to facilitate quick wardrobe changes between events. As such, the Queen has often had to sacrifice personal taste and fashionability in favour of practicality. But while she has persistently favoured a wardrobe of matching dresses and coats, she has often expressed her personality through her choice of hats. In the early years of her reign, she wore hats made by milliner Aage Thaarup, from whom she chose pieces 'topped with huge velvet bows, mammoth roses or an outsize daisy, a feather pompom or even a whole

11. Buruma, p.17

"A Stephen Jones hat is like a William Hogarth painting — a deeply shrewd portrait of England and its eccentricities. Punks, cricket, football, the Queen, the Union Jack, the London Underground, and even fish and chips and cups of tea have all been placed under Stephen's anthropological microscope. But Stephen's patriotic millinery extends beyond iconography to one of the fundamental characteristics of Englishness, namely a love of extremes, a love that expresses itself through satire and irony, English literary traditions that are the hallmarks of Stephen's dazzling creativity and dexterous conceptualism."

ANDREW BOLTON

bird'.[12] By the time Jones came to millinery, however, the Queen was in her 50s and her youthful selection of hats had settled into signature Breton styles, neat turbans and toques perched on top of her head. Nonetheless, her style has had a very strong national presence and Jones feels that 'the Queen is absolutely still a measure for being "properly" attired today'.[13]

In 1981, another royal influence bolstered the British millinery industry in the guise of the new Princess of Wales, formerly Lady Diana Spencer. Young and attractive, with access to top fashion designers, Princess Diana quickly became a style icon. As royal protocol required that she wear hats, her patronage had a huge impact on the millinery industry. Her choice of honeymoon hat — a simple tricorn with an ostrich feather, designed by John Boyd — created an unprecedented demand for copies across the country. Suddenly the hat was once again an important accessory in the wardrobe of the British woman. Jones was soon invited to design a hat for the young Princess, who loved the resulting beret and ordered several versions. In 1982, Jones's work appeared on the cover of the British society magazine *Tatler*, and the Victoria and Albert Museum, London, approached him in order to acquire the hat for their collections of dress and fashion. Jones was now firmly established within the British millinery scene.

The foremost British milliners of the 20th century were a vibrant, eccentric and whimsical group who used their hats to push boundaries and add an irreverent touch to the formal wardrobes of many women. Taking inspiration from objects and ideas, both familiar and obscure, they turned their diverse source material into hats. Jones follows in this tradition. Surprisingly, a number of these noted milliners came from abroad to set up their businesses amongst a receptive British audience. Aage Thaarup, a Danish milliner, dressed the young Queen in lavishly decorated light-hearted bonnets and caps. He also edited his own magazine, *Pinpoints*, which ran for four issues in 1939. This fun and frivolous publication discussed British art, literature and fashion, and was notable for its illustrated advertisements and hand-tinted pages. French émigrée Simone Mirman was another foreign milliner who made hats for the Queen and Princess Margaret. Known for her fanciful creations, she used the finest materials and skills to create humorous hats with striking and surprising silhouettes. The highly regarded Frederick Fox, also a royal milliner, hailed originally from Australia. Arriving from abroad, these milliners may have had the advantage of a detached eye better able to identify and exploit the British love for capricious and humorous hats; or it may be that living and working within Britain they simply were quick to absorb the national appreciation of *whimsy*.

Top: *Tatler* magazine cover, featuring *Tit-Tat*, which is the common name for the magazine. The shape of the hat takes its inspiration from the famous Tatlin Tower. Styled by Michael Roberts.

Below: Stephen Jones at the Japanese department store Isetan for his 1984 exhibition, posing with a portrait of Diana, Princess of Wales, wearing a suede beret by Stephen Jones for Jasper Conran.

Left: 26th February 1947, Cape Town, South Africa, Princess Elizabeth (later Queen Elizabeth II) and Princess Margaret followed by the Queen, later the Queen Mother, at the Kenilworth racecourse during their tour of South Africa.

12. Edwards, Anne, *The Queen's Clothes* (London, 1977), p.14

13. Stephen Jones interview with Oriole Cullen (18.05.2010)

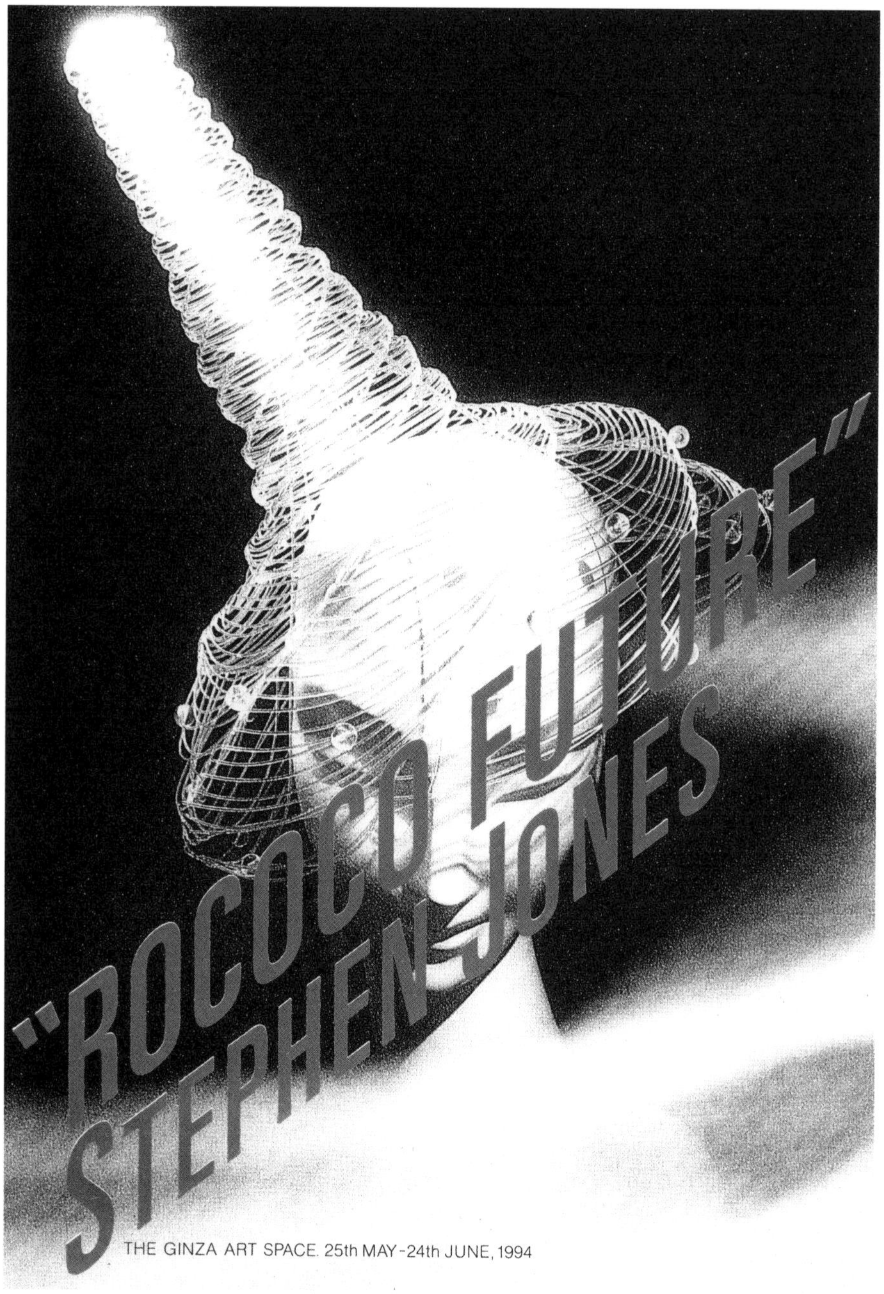

Top: Invitation for the *Rococo Future* exhibition at the Ginza Art Space, Tokyo, 1994.
Hat fashioned from plastic in a traditional straw plaiting technique.

Right: Stella Tennant wearing a Stephen Jones hat in tulle, in the shape of a christmas tree, A/W 1996–97.

Vibe, S/S 1998. Hat from laize and canes, inspired by British sculptor Barbara Hepworth. MoMu Collection B02/38.

If the design of hats can be typically identified as British, so too can the techniques used by the nation's milliners. When Jones first started working with French milliners in his Parisian atelier at Christian Dior, they were astounded at the differences in practices; many of the methods Jones employs having long gone out of use in France. Jones believes British hats – particularly his own and those of Philip Treacy – bring a lightness of touch and a sense of whimsy to the Parisian collections. His spring–summer 2005 collection was inspired by English eccentricity. Hats such as *May Queen* (a floral wreath of glass beads), *Regatta* (a straw boater) and *Presentation* (a plastic tiara) all highlighted notions of English heritage, while the title of the collection, *Handmade in England*, underlined the expertise and craft with which a Stephen Jones hat is made.

Passing skills from generation to generation is a key tradition in British millinery. The inimitable Shirley Hex, tutor to both Jones and Treacy, spent many years instructing apprentices whilst head of several high profile millinery ateliers, including those at Lachasse and Frederick Fox. She then went on to run the postgraduate millinery course at the Royal College of Art until the 1990s. Hex learnt her trade as an apprentice at millinery firm Edward Mann. At the time, she wished she was working at Madame Vernier, a firm that had more connotations of French chic; she could not have foreseen how her influence and her star pupils would later make Britain the international centre of the millinery world.

Stephen Jones embodies the extremes of Britishness in his ability to seamlessly combine elements of rebellion with the Establishment. Even when attired in morning dress to receive his OBE at Buckingham Palace, he still insisted on a touch of punk, wearing a silver watch chain that resembled barbed wire. Jones attended a traditional British boarding school – where he recalls, half-jokingly, they were taught 'to play rugby and rule the Empire' [14] – yet he came of age in postcolonial Britain when race, sexuality, music and style were all merging together in the club scene of the early 1980s. He notes, 'I experienced firsthand new youth movements which offered a whimsical reaction to the seriousness, banality or politicization of the status quo'. [15] With his immaculate manners, charm and unique personal style, Jones is the personification of the modern British gentleman. He merges his love for all things traditional with a quick and discerning eye for the contemporary, rendering his work continually fresh and relevant. For Jones, the hats he creates are an extension of the life he leads, and perhaps therein lies the essence of the British touch.

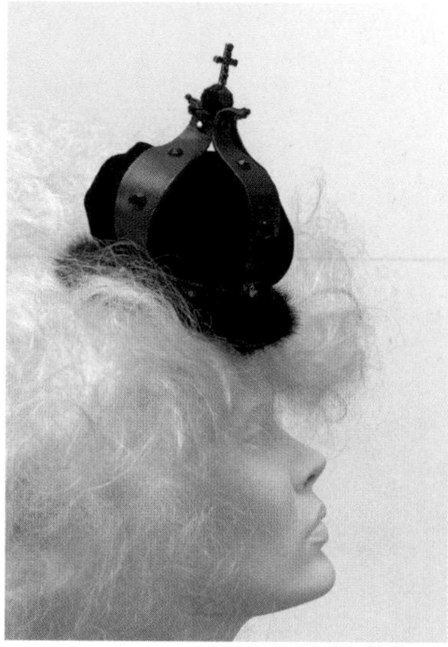

Top: *Zuleika*, A/W 2001–02

Right: *Myra*, A/W 2003–04
Inspired by Myra, a friend from Jones's time at the Blitz club, who wore a doll's face in her beehive hairdo.

14. Stephen Jones interview with Oriole Cullen (01.04.2010)

15. Jones (2006), p.5

"Dita has dressed like an Agatha Christie heroine in Moschino's tattersall cape and pumpkin taffeta blouse and Stephen Jones's minature feather top hat with a tail of arching plumes.
– 'That looks very much like a pheasant!' says the bird handler as his hawks greedily eye her headgear." HAMISH BOWLES

Top: Dita Von Teese, wearing a Stephen Jones hat with pheasant feathers, at Castle Gurteen Le Poer in Kilsheelan, County Tipperary, Ireland. December 2005. Published in *Vogue* US, March 2006.

Right: *Heel*, A/W 2009–10
Hat with the sole of a Dr Martens boot, supported by a Union Jack matchbox.
MoMu Collection B 10/41

MADE IN ENGLAND

Stephen Jones & Solve Sundsbo. Special commission, London, 2010. *Trawler*, S/S 1987

STEPHEN JONES & THE PHOTOGRAPHIC IMAGE

Magdalene Keaney
Curator, Fashion Space Gallery,
London College of Fashion

Steve Strange discusses the detailing on a £1000 suit and hat with Antony Price.

— AP: 'Grey silk-braid piping on black leather.'
— SS: 'Perfect for photographic work.'
— AP: 'That's all that counts in our world.'

'This Hectic Life', Miles Chapman, *Tatler* – March 1982

Almost all of what I know about Stephen Jones, I know via photography. I formerly worked at the National Portrait Gallery (NPG), London, and a striking black and white portrait of the milliner by Nick Knight remains among my personal favourites in the photographic collection. Knight's portrait shows a man of unquestionable elegance but operates as a playful tease rather than a full-blown physical revelation. The image, part of the photographer's now seminal group of 100 portraits taken for *i-D* magazine in 1985, introduces three key ideas in this essay: first, that photographic portraits of Jones are but one of several strands of images around the man and his hats, and that, in some way, these images have *become* the man and his hats; second, that Jones's long-standing relationships with specific photographers – including Nick Knight, Peter Ashworth, Paolo Roversi, Sølve Sundsbø and Mario Testino – have resulted in pictures with the potential to transform Jones's work; third, that the emergence and flourishing of such style magazines as *The Face* and *i-D* made for key platforms in Jones's early career.

Over a 30 year period, Jones and his hats have appeared in many different kinds of images, both still and moving. These include celebrity portraits, fashion stories, still life and beauty photography, music videos, feature films, album covers, social documentary, paparazzi snaps and end of cat-

Stephen Jones & Sølve Sundsbø
Special commission, London, 2010.
Soho, A/W 1998–99

In this
Style
€10

Natalia Vodianova, Stephen Jones and Christian Lacroix in a shoot inspired by *Alice in Wonderland*; Stephen Jones as the Mad Hatter', *Vogue* US, 2003.

Miffi wearing felt hood shaped like a 2. Part of a series of numeral clothes from 1–10. Commissioned by Kim Bowen for *Blitz* magazine, September 1990.

"So often a hat will vie for control of a fashion image, dominating all communication with a devastating one-liner. By contrast, Stephen Jones' hats are more like a fantastically versatile system of punctuation. Sometimes they link together disparate elements, sometimes they finesse rough or angular ones and occasionally, they make surprising statements of their own. But most frequently, they represent the definitive full stop."

PENNY MARTIN

Michelle Hicks wearing *Icarus*, A/W 1995–96, published in *The Face*. A single plume contrived from ostrich and turkey feathers for extra drama.

walk pictures. For most of us who will never own or perhaps even pick up a Stephen Jones hat, the image *is* the hat. For example, a girl growing up in the 1980s in a small city in Australia – probably as geographically and culturally removed from the world of Stephen Jones as one could be — is an ardent fan of Culture Club. Jones, who at one time lived with Boy George, often designed hats for the singer and appeared in the video for 'Do You Really Want to Hurt Me?'. He made a particular style of black hat worn by Boy George — a bowler — that this girl dreams of wearing, though she does not know who Stephen Jones is, much less that he makes these hats. Thus, aged nine, what she thought was a Culture Club moment, maybe considered a bit of an exotic London moment, was equally a Stephen Jones moment (which it takes her a further 28 years to figure out).

Jones's iconography is significant and weaves between many genres, styles and functions. In a second portrait in the NPG collection shot by Steve Speller, Jones appears as statuary. All angles in pose and profile, here he is an Egyptian hieroglyphic. The meaning of the symbol is unmistakable — style. An Annie Leibovitz photograph of Jones depicts a fashion fantasy: a garden party from *Alice's Adventures in Wonderland* with the milliner cast as the mad hatter (wearing a splendid top hat and matching suit, although in Sir John Tenniel's original illustrations it is the White Rabbit who wears a check suit); Natalia Vodianova reclines as a languid Alice, and Christian Lacroix poses as the March Hare. In a photograph by Angus McBean, Jones becomes his art; wrapped in tissue, presented in a Stephen Jones hat box and wearing a Stephen Jones hat. The image displays the surrealist sensibility and humour for which McBean was well known, and which run close to Jones's own aesthetic tastes. In this case, the hat quite literally fits *and* he wears it.

Social documentary and snapshots from the 1980s are less 'official' than the portraits mentioned above, but no less important when considering images of the milliner. Photographs show Jones at Blitz nightclub, with staff in his first shop, at parties and openings, making final adjustments to models before a fashion show; there are many hundreds of such images in existence. More likely to be dug out of the back of a drawer than collected by a museum, they nonetheless provide incredibly valuable — and downright fabulous — historical and contextual information about Jones and his milieu. Going out was inextricably linked to fashion and performance among Jones's social circle, and the headdress needs of his friends, and, of course, also his own, were important catalysts to the creation and presentation of his hats. But, as Jones tells me, the event was often not the actual wearing of the hat, but the photo showing the hat being worn.

Stephen Jones hats also become an event when photographed on celebrities at premieres and red carpet events. Here again, you are likely to have

Stephen Jones wearing *Waimea*, S/S 1998, designed on Waimea beach, North Shore Hawaii.

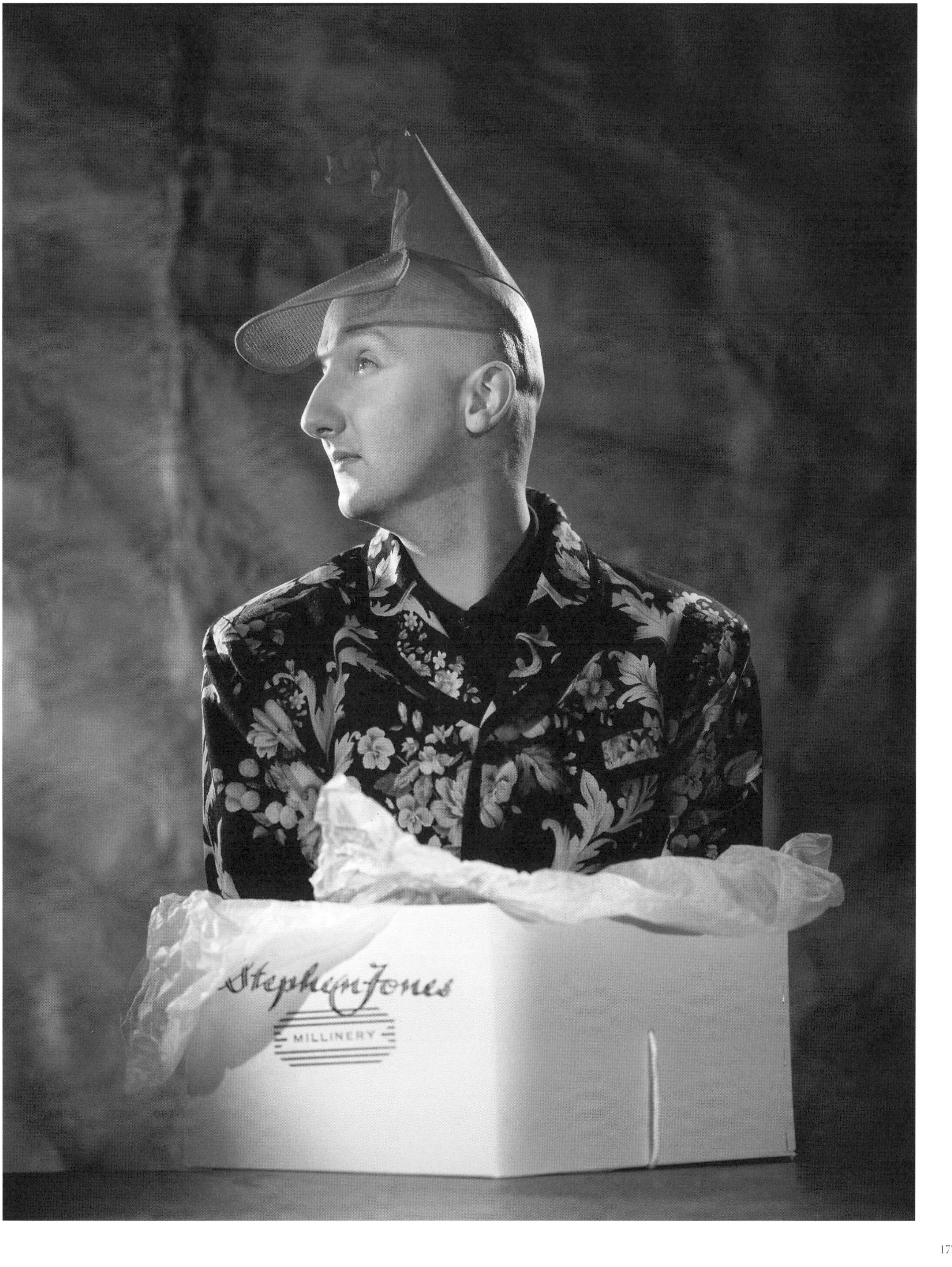
Stephen Jones
MILLINERY

Venus, *Superior*, *Persian Baroque*, *Shoal* & *Beachcomber* from the S/S 2001 collection, *Icon*. Studio test with Stephen Jones's team.

Venus, *Superior*, *Persian Baroque*, *Shoal* & *Beachcomber* from the S/S 2001 collection, *Icon*. Invitation.

Top: Kate Moss at the Costume Institute Gala 2009 at the Metropolitan Museum, NY, wearing a gold lamé Marc Jacobs dress and a Stephen Jones turban.

Left: *Electra*, A/W 2006–07 MoMu Collection B08/19

a Stephen Jones moment without actually knowing it at the time. So, for instance, when Kate Moss attended the 2009 Metropolitan Museum of Art's annual Costume Institute Gala in New York, we all instantly recognized her in the images that dominated daily newspapers and blogs following the event. What I did not know was that the knockout gold turban she wore — I wondered if we would see copies on the high street later that season — was by Stephen Jones.

Fashion photography has been an important source of inspiration for Jones since he was a student. Though he personally related to a punk sensibility, he located British *Vogue* magazines from the 1940s and 1950s in the library at St Martin's School of Art and discovered the work of Norman Parkinson, John French, Horst P Horst, Angus McBean and David Bailey. Purchasing a copy of Georgina Howell's *In Vogue: Six Decades of Fashion* was a hefty financial outlay for the young hat maker but one that he gladly made. The book became a treasured visual compendium and assisted the cultivation of Jones's own vision. Cecil Beaton became a hero, and whilst we talk, Jones also shows me the work of Regina Relang, another favourite photographer.

It is important to try to pin down how Jones's designs operate as part of a fashion image. What do they contribute? What is the relationship between the designer, his hats, the photographer and the final image? Fashion photographers are first and foremost photographers — image-makers. They apply their chosen medium to an array of specialized subgenres, including fashion editorials — Matt Irwin photographed Stephen Jones for Walter Van Beirendonck; fashion advertising — Juergen Teller shot Victoria Beckham in Stephen Jones for Marc Jacobs; beauty shots — Ben Hassett captured Jones's *Trumpet* hat in a hair feature; still life — Jason Pietracatella snapped Stephen Jones perfume; and so on. The resulting photographs are defined by the subject (a fashion or design object however abstract), intent (the desire to communicate in some way about the subject, often related to commerce) and process (which usually involves a team of people, including a stylist). When a fashion photograph is more than a functional commercial document, the result can be powerful and original creative expression — the fashion photograph as art — though this does not negate its underlying commercial purpose. The subject, in this case a hat by Stephen Jones, remains intrinsic but is to varying degrees sublimated to the whole; to the photographer's own process and the resulting aesthetic outcome.

Jones established himself in London concurrent with several of the photographers he continues to work with, including Mario Testino and Nick Knight, both of whom have become as highly regarded in their field as

Victoria Beckham wearing the Marc Jacobs version of *Le Dix*. Marc Jacobs Campaign S/S 2008, *Legs, Bag and Shoes*, LA 2007.

Stephen Jones & Comme des Garçons, 2008. The concept for the perfume is 'A violet hit by a meteorite'. The shape is inspired by an ink bottle of the 1890s.

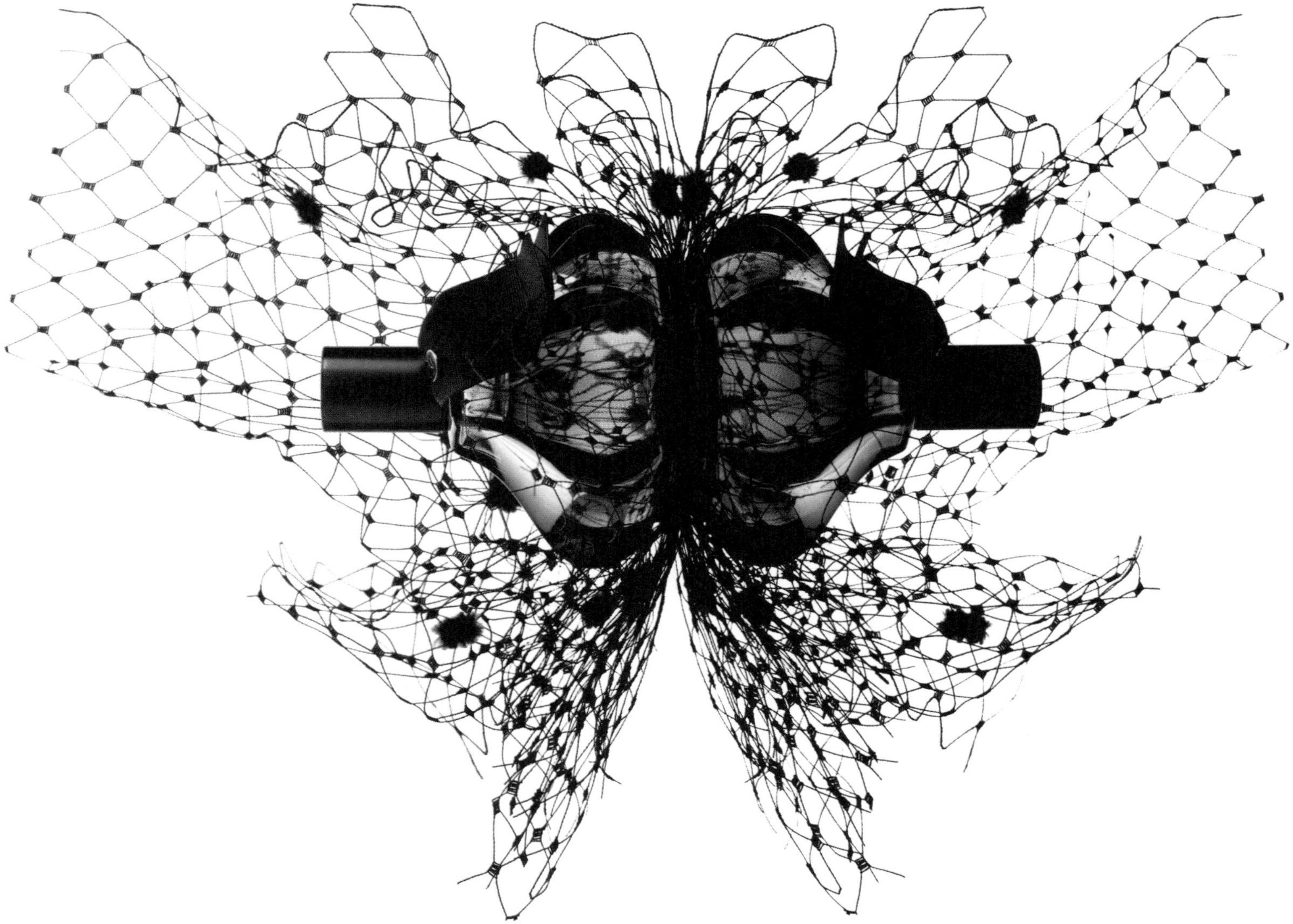

Top: *Zephyr*, S/S 1984
Make-up by Phyllis Cohen.

Left: Nun's coif inspired by the 'Tourterelles Immaculées' in Federico Fellini's 1972 film *Roma*.
Special commission for *POP* magazine, Autumn Issue September 2008.

Top: Mario Testino's first published photograph in *Ms London* magazine, featuring a Stephen Jones hat, 6 May 1980.

Bottom: Cate Blanchett wearing a plumed helmet by Stephen Jones for Christian Dior Haute Couture, A/W 2006–07, in *Vogue* US, November 2006.

Left: Designer Gareth Pugh styled by Katie Grand, in a Giles ostrich spine headdress, *Arena Homme Plus*, 2007.

Jones has in his. I doubt any of the three would have imagined the stellar heights awaiting them. In 2002, Testino – whose first published photograph in *Ms London* magazine (6 May 1980), featured a Stephen Jones hat – staged one of the most popular exhibitions ever at the NPG. Knight, who first photographed Jones back in 1985, became one of the preeminent photographers of his time, and in 2001 produced a Stephen Jones postage stamp for the Royal Mail. Working your way up through the ranks together is an important dynamic in the fashion world, where collaboration underpins the photographer's image-making. Those photographers and stylists who know Jones personally can telephone him with ideas for a fashion editorial (the subgenre of fashion photography that I would argue allows the most creative freedom) and the milliner will translate the story's concept into a specific piece. He will sometimes then attend the shoot himself to style and position the hat on the model. In other cases, magazine editors will request hats either as the key piece presented in the fashion image – such as in the case of Steven Klein's magnificent plumed helmet by Jones – or to complement and push a look they are exploring for the season. In a photo by David Sims, Jones's creation adds both height and another layer of textural detail. Here the hat is very much integrated within the whole look to the point of actually being entwined with the model's hair.

Sølve Sundsbø is a frequent photographer of Stephen Jones hats. He is known for what I think of as 'experimental perfectionism' and Jones tells me he admires Sundsbø's abstract and transformative interpretations of his hats. In the 2007 editorial 'Batty Boy' for *Arena Homme Plus*, the pared-down studio setting and chiaroscuro emphasize the structure of designer Gareth Pugh's distinctive features and the monochrome fashions brilliantly styled by Katie Grand. The latter composes fashion in photographs as originally and with as much sophistication as a photographer creating a visual or graphic language. In several images, a head-based flourish is set against simple geometric shapes and dark silhouettes on the body. In one shot, a spherical headpiece by Jones – made as part of a collection for the designer Giles – is photographed in profile. Taking on a life of its own, the hat appears as an indefinable, orbiting live energy. Contrasting segments in the wired strands reflect glints of light. Jones theorizes that photography makes hats believable. He says this fully aware of the apparent contradiction in this belief since in a fashion photograph nothing is left to chance; everything is an artifice. Jones finds this artifice exciting.

In 1980, *The Face* described Jones's art as 'hats to build a wardrobe around, almost hats to build a lifestyle around'. They are certainly hats to build an image around. Obvious examples include the photographs of Peter Lindbergh or Steven Meisel in which the hat becomes the central motif of the image, accentuated by a close crop, the use of colour or the

Top left: *Vanity Fair* cover, January 2009, commissioned by Michael Roberts.
Top right: Gwen Stefani wearing *Concorde* in satin and rhinestones by Stephen Jones for Marc Jacobs, *V* magazine N°52, March 2008.

Right: *Doppler*, S/S 1998. Hat in stitched organza.

Gemma Ward wearing *Big Pansy*, British *Vogue*, March 2004.

visual centrality of the shape or angle of the hat. Alice Springs's portrait of Anjelica Huston is a less obvious example, but the line and shape of Jones's piece, though not large in the composition, still commands our attention. Pulling our eye straight to Huston's face, it also playfully verges on upstaging the sophistication and strength of the actress's renowned profile.

If you are an emerging fashion designer, prestige and commercial opportunity can be conferred by a well-known photographer or stylist picking up on your work. While Jones was still establishing his reputation, his hats captured the eye and heart of Paolo Roversi, already an influential and highly regarded photographer living in Paris. There is a beautiful synergy in how a Jones hat appears seamlessly in a Roversi image, often like a mood or premonition rather than a physical object. More recently, David Bailey's portrait of Anna Piaggi signals Jones's stature within the industry. Piaggi is a contemporary fashion icon and her too small, off-kilter hat by Jones is her trademark.

'You do think [about] how is it going to look on the cover of *Vogue*', Jones tells me close to the end of our discussion. The *Vogue* cover, almost always a photograph, is the endorsement of the fashion Establishment. Since 1983, Jones's hats have appeared on the cover of *Vogue* many times. Other significant early editorials include his first cover for *Tatler* shot by Terence Donovan in 1982, and an early story for *Harpers & Queen*, put together by Hamish Bowles, then a 19-year-old fashion director, and photographed by Clive Arrowsmith. Though these mastheads are revered and powerful fashion institutions, surely the most noteworthy (and loved) of Jones's covers appeared on a magazine that sought to subvert the weight and stagnation of the English Establishment. Commissioned in 1985 to front the 5th anniversary issue of *i-D* magazine, the photograph by Nick Knight is a tribute to Vivienne Westwood, to London, to punk and to Jones. The cover heralds the ascendance of a new generation of writers, photographers, artists, musicians and designers – Jones's generation. Royalty had never been so cool, British fashion had rarely been so confident and celebratory. Stephen Jones crowned the moment and Knight ensured it was one we will never forget.

BIBLIOGRAPHY
Georgina Howell, *In Vogue: Six Decades of Fashion*, London: Allen Lane, 1975.

Right: *Peony Girls*, MAC cosmetics campaign for China. The models were nude with bodypainting, simulating traditional *qipao* dress, 2005.

Left: *Profile*, S/S 2001, *Hanatsubaki* magazine #636, published by Shiseido, 2003.

Left: Stephen Jones for Giles
Headdress with ostrich feathers, S/S 2007.

Right: Clara Aker Benjamin wearing
Serengeti 1935, A/W 1997–98.
MoMu Collection B02/45

Past, Present and Couture. Christian Dior Haute Couture A/W 2001–02, *Hill Tribe* headdress with embroidery, aluminium and coyote.

Seagull, S/S 1996

Harper's Bazaar cover featuring *Chilli* hat. Illustration by Tony Viramontes, October 1984.

Top left: Hat in embroidered cotton for a Twix advertisement, 'Twix fits', 1989.
Top right: Hat in resin, simulating splashing water, for a Perrier advertisement, *In Veaugue, Perrier, official mineral water of London Fashion Week*, October 1995.

Right: Stephen Jones in a spoof advert for Shiseido in *Hanatsubaki* magazine #532, published by Shiseido, 1994.

space products
hair
in a tube

STEPHEN JONES & RESEARCH

Judith Clark
Exhibition-maker and Reader in the Field of Fashion and Museology, London College of Fashion

'... & then you find it here'

Research is about expanding a repertoire of references. It is about finding imagery or ideas that are fed into and are translated by a private idiom. Sometimes in the process they become indiscernible, unrecognizable. Sometimes references are simply edited out, rejected. Some are part of trajectories – stepping stones to better ideas that worked, and ultimately, for Stephen Jones, research is about his way of designing a good hat.

The trail, that unused, un-translated research leaves behind is what Stephen Jones calls his 'general knowledge'. The range and scope of these references and allusions are extraordinary. He seems to be writing a new kind of history by making hats; like Claude Lévi-Strauss's *bricoleur*, he uses what is to hand with incredible instinct. We know he has had all the fun. That in order to find the right colours for a hat's lining, he has travelled to the Norton Simon Museum in Pasadena, where he has matched the lining to the draped robes of the *trompe l'œil* figures in Giovanni Battista Tiepolo's *The Triumph of Virtue and Nobility Over Ignorance* (painted originally as a design for the ceiling of Palazzo Manin, Venice); that such was his desire to follow Tiepolo's path for his last collection (entitled simply *XYZ*), that he then travelled to visit the artist's Bavarian interiors, finally deciding to marry these with Man Ray's x-ray photographs and, following a short stay in hospital, surgical face masks.

Jones's attitude resists earnestness, as though his research is a series of lucky finds, the experience one has sometimes when browsing in a secondhand bookshop. He cherishes his eccentric lightness of touch and relishes his prerogative as a designer (rather than an academic) to abandon one line of enquiry at the moment something else catches his eye. What happens, however, when you stare at something for long enough is that you begin to notice preoccupations, resonances and 'workings out'; in Jones's case, this is his general knowledge at work.

Stephen Jones & Paolo Roversi
Special commission, Paris, 2010

Ecstasy, S/S 2007. Photoprint on satin of a close-up of a delirious Moira Shearer in the surreal ballet sequence of Pressburger and Powell's 1948 dance film *The Red Shoes*.

Season's mood board showing inspirations for S/S 2007 collection *Artifice*.

THE RED SHOES
MARK CONNELLY
TURNER CLASSIC MOVIES

'... & then you find it here'

Repetitions and recurrences, coincidences and overlaps, organise Jones's research. Like literary critic Christopher Ricks's recall of recurring words across poems and between poets, Jones uses images, or even chance meetings, as symbolic connections. The sentence '... and then you find it here' came up a lot when I spoke to Jones recently about his research for his spring–summer 2011 collection. It seemed to be absolutely essential to what we were discussing; proof along the way that he was going in the right direction — that something he had discovered was already embedded within the next step, that his hunch had been right all along.

Whilst I write this piece, the spring–summer 2011 collection is still a long way off. The excitement of discussing a project so far in advance is that the research is still new and, importantly, it is still around. It has not yet been edited down; it has momentum. As with all Stephen Jones collections, a library has begun to grow within the larger library at his Covent Garden studio. A small side table, tucked behind the door of the studio library, is his temporary 'current bookcase'. Jones mainly keeps any books relevant to the collection there, but some, more precious ones, are kept at home. These books either fall under a few specific subjects, such as interiors, Polynesian art and Pacifica, or they have beautiful bindings: a series of books from the 1940s with two-colour bindings; a first edition of Vita Sackville-West's *In Your Garden*, and the wonderful book of *Flair* Magazine. More books, of course, are stacked by his bedside.

His books act as a bibliography to each collection. What is impossible to discern without his guidance, however, is what they have in common. He is less interested in subject matter, more interested in nuance, tone, depth of field; an awkward composition — a 'Margaret Rutherford-ness'; in those aspects that spark his imagination but pass most of us by. So the books do not conform to one period, for example, or even a consensual sense of taste, but they are fundamental nonetheless; the fonts used on a page, the specific pages or the binding might be key, making it absolutely essential that it be *that* book, *that* edition, *that* year. And, whilst a collection is on his mind, that small library travels with him; sometimes whole books come, sometimes only photocopies of specific pages.

'I thought — 'why is this about books?' And I had just unpacked my case that I had at the weekend and here is *Polyhedra in Origami*, Mark Holborn's *Irving Penn Regards the Work of Issey Miyake*, a flower-arranging book from Kent County Council, *Origami, The Art of Flower Arranging* — [a] fabulous, fabulous late 1950s book, which is when they [were] assimilating Japanese concepts of beauty into western ideas —

Below: Fleur Cowles (ed.), *The Best of Flair magazine*, Scriptum Editions & Cartago, London, 1999.

Right: Collage for A/W collection *XYZ*, featuring a painting by Giovanni Battista Tiepolo, *The Triumph of Virtue*, c. 1740–1750. Oil on canvas (Ceiling painting for the Palazzo Manin, Venice), The Norton Simon Foundation, F.1972.26.P.

Lillian Bassman

Tiepolo

Man Ray.

Marion Adnams
L'Infante Egarée (The Distraught Infanta), 1944
Oil on panel
Manchester Art Gallery

Norman De Kalb Edwards, *The Art of Flower Arrangement*, Viking Press, New York, 1961.

anyway, *The Poetry of Crisis: The Peter Nahum Collection of British Surrealist and Avant-Garde Art, 1930–1951* (a Christie's catalogue from November 2006), ...

Last Christmas, Jones travelled to Manchester to visit the exhibition *Angels of Anarchy: Women Artists and Surrealism* at the Manchester Art Gallery. It included work by Frida Kahlo, Lee Miller, Meret Oppenheim and Leonora Carrington, as well as more recent pieces by artists such as Francesca Woodman. The work that really struck him, however, was that of the lesser known British artist Marion Adnams:

'She did these really amazing paintings ... some of her paintings were dolls made out of paper, 'origami-esque', and then she painted them in scenes. She was a British Surrealist during the 1930s. What I loved about [her work] was its 'Englishness' – [it was] slightly useless. In France it would have been challenging; if she had been Italian it would have been beautifully decorative; but it is somehow English. And she was an art teacher... as her sight went she would get bits of driftwood and nail them on the walls and they were the most beautiful things ever, and she would do drawings of them as well. And from that I started to look into – and this is a book that I bought in New York – *The Art of Flower Arrangement*, which is when they started to use driftwood, and it arrived today [he laughs]. And this one is from Borneo and this one from Sumatra ... and I found this book of poems by Alison Brackenbury who has used the Marion Adnams painting on the cover ...

Jones's research emerges as a wonderful stream of consciousness and free association. It is only the second time that he has become so preoccupied with one individual to drive the beginnings of his research. The first was Duchesa Simonetta Colonna di Cesaro who became his muse for *La Prima Donna*, his autumn–winter 2004–05 collection. But that was an homage to a living fashion designer, whom he had met, spent time with, and looked through many representations of; with Adnams it is different. It is about someone's relentlessly British work produced within the sensual milieu of European Surrealism; about someone who was in many ways as unglamorous as Simonetta, a member of the Roman aristocracy, is glamorous. But maybe, as such, Adnams is just as exotic to Jones. He looked at her painting *Aftermath*: 'Can you see how it is very English? Barbed wire from the war ... a skull with a bow on it! I love the fact that it is a skull with a bow on it. If it were Frida Kahlo it wouldn't have a bow on it – I love the fact that it is so dysfunctionally British ...'

These are not the kind of references that anyone might look up – it is about looking; looking at the actual painting and recognizing its oddities. One of the astonishing things about my conversation with Jones was how

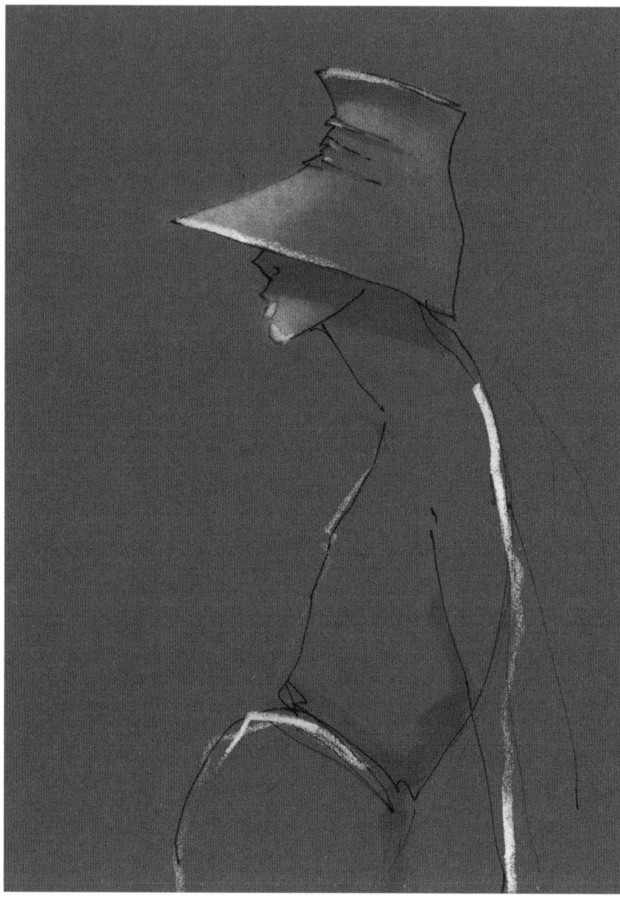

Clockwise from top left: *Moroccan Bizarre*, S/S 1994; *Farah*, S/S 1993; *Fairness*, S/S 1988 & *M.T.V.*, A/W 1993–94.

Drawing of *Musical*, A/W 1992 93

often the jumps that are so personal and so integral to his itinerant lifestyle are so utterly unexpected. And as so much of his work is associative it is therefore invisible. Driftwood from Adnams' compositions by now has become drifting, drifting as something that is not positive, that is somehow nebulous and it is associated not so much only with the wood itself but with an environment. *Drifting &* is the preliminary title of the next collection (even the ampersand itself, its graphic outline is active for Jones, referential to this exhibition at MoMu, and one cannot help but think of recent work at the Victoria and Albert Museum)[1] and it moves it into another stage.

During his research, Jones shifted his attention from the cherished object in the painting's foreground to its darker background, which he (out of nowhere but as though entirely logical and sequential) traced back to being on Howe Island, where he downloaded Brian Eno's album *Another Green World* from iTunes. The music encouraged his thoughts on Adnams' work which he concluded is very much about background and foreground – the former being a bit surreal, the latter being the thing she had made (the craft object) – and that somehow there is also a middle ground, which is about texture.

'There seem to be three different influences: there seems to be Marion Adnams, [who] I am fascinated by, and amazed at her work and that she was an unsung hero; and [there's] that Englishness ... a bit Margaret Rutherford – she could have been in *Blithe Spirit* as Madame Arcati, she could have been her artistic cousin; and there is Miyake. There is something very 'mid-ground' about [all of] them.'

His research has become a total world, like an exhibition, inhabited by characters, and it is definitively in three dimensions. Jones is preoccupied with curating, with visualizing his hats in museums; could his dreamscape be the positioning of his hats in an environment?

'... and what I want to do is build a stage set. I want to make something like you would find in a Treviso local museum, like an illustration of America being discovered ... with a diorama in the background that is badly painted. I want to make that and that's why I bought the pieces of driftwood. [They are] going to somehow be my mid-ground which is [based around] Miyake, and I will make some paper sculpture of some description and that thing ... is going to be the inspiration for the collection. It could be physically oil paint or something like that and there will be bits of wood and bits of paper – but actual hats. I don't really know yet ... I would like them to have a strange ethereal beauty from [which] I might get an unusual macabre quality. The challenge will be to make it [the collection] non-specific. It will be a challenge this season to make things which are not specific, not positive in a way, working within a lot of non-precision.

Top: *Paper Girl* drawing by Marion Adnams.

Right: Sketch for *Top Hat*, S/S 2011

1. *Hats: An Anthology by Stephen Jones*, Victoria and Albert Museum, London (24 February–31 May 2009); Its title references *Fashion: An Anthology by Cecil Beaton* which was held at the V&A in 1971 and helped put fashion on the museum's agenda.

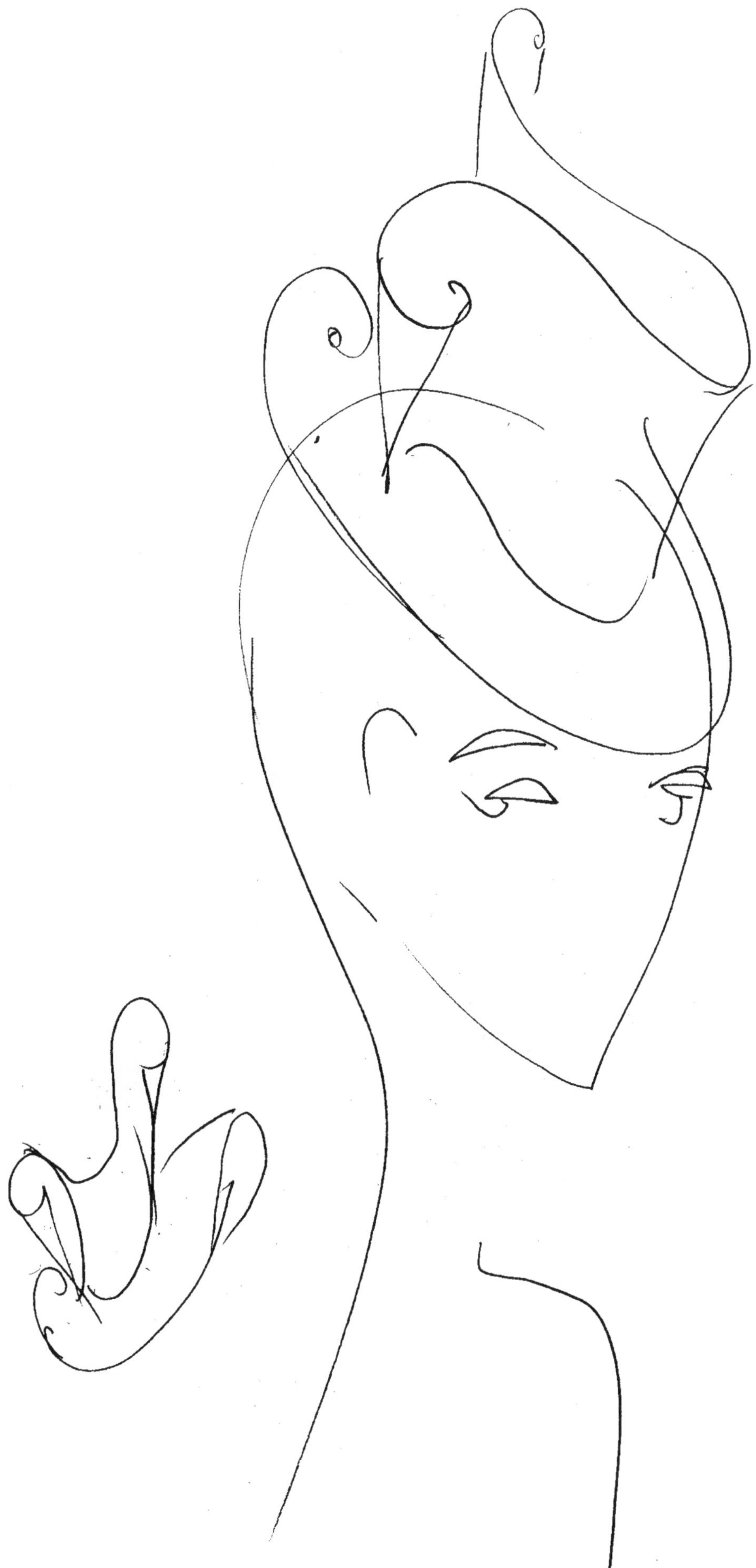

Spirit Drifting
Curled turkey feathers
or tulle - sinamay? wire frame.
grey + peach
C
curl.

Natasha Kroll, *Window Display*, Studio Publications, London, 1954.

Sketch for *Spirits Drifting*, S/S 2011

I can't really explain, and if I could explain it would be done. I need to find out. One thing that I know … is … how those different themes fit together in the actual hat and the way of showing them — if it were one, two, three, we would not have all ones at the beginning, we would have one, two, three, one, two, three — the rhythm, the hats might set up a rhythm, like a musical rhythm … You might have something [a hat] which is very much … close-up and in focus, and then one that is totally about texture.'

We discussed the paper folding sculptures, origami, and Jones's resistance to them becoming too doll-like, but the sculptures seemed mannequin-like to me. I was thinking of the books in his broader library that were standing by, as though just in case — just in case he needed an emergency reference. I was thinking of his books from the 1950s and how so many of them have photographs of those paper dolls then used in shop displays and those awkward backdrops that featured behind glamorous dresses mounted on paper cut-outs. But anything figurative at this stage seemed too literal for Jones, as if it was too late for that in his research; that somehow Marion Adnams was no longer simply Marion Adnams but 'Adnams + Miyake + Eno', a contemporary collection in which dolls would just not fit.

We spoke again of books and why they are so important to Jones, as a passion that has run throughout his working life and that has simply been made more efficient — by Google and Amazon, perhaps. Books have clearly become synonymous with different periods in his life; Georgina Howells's *In Vogue*, for example, which he bought for a term's money, gave him a glimpse of the breadth of design possibilities open to him; others include the *American Fashion* book, which he stole from the St Martin's School of Art library, together with Diana Vreeland's *Romantic and Glamorous Hollywood Design*, 1974 exhibition catalogue from the Metropolitan Museum of Art's Costume Institute in New York. I asked Jones why he could not part with these two books and he said it was about adrenalin, that they were the most exciting things he had ever seen in his life: '… it's a cover. I prefer second-hand. I like a ripped dust jacket, and some funny marking; I love a thumbprint or a fiver.'

Jones has built up his library over many years but, as indicated by his current preoccupations, it is not about dress histories (even though those remain a central love of his); it *is* science meets glamour meets adventure meets rococo; it includes biographies, anthologies, dictionaries, surveys and museologies.

The idea of 'metamorphosis' came to mind when looking at his books — that somehow women could be transformed into any of the objects and

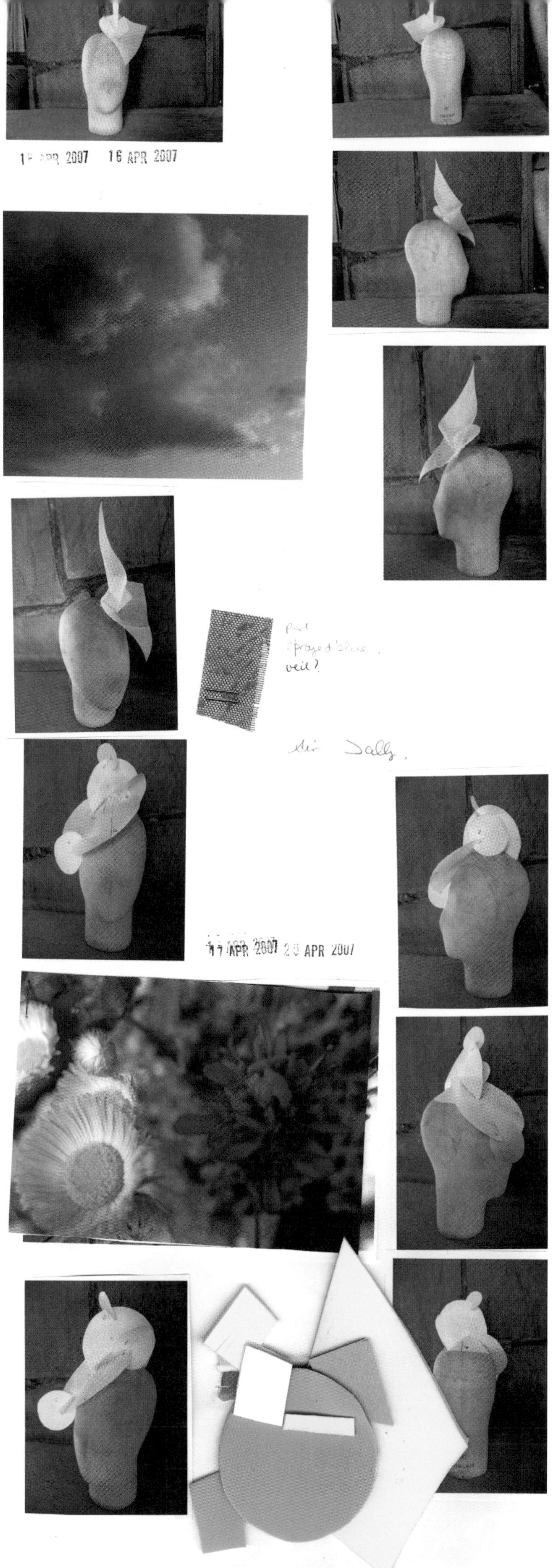

Invitation for S/S 2008 collection *Desert Rose*, inspired by a trip to Southern Utah.

Inspirations and toiles designed on Trees Ranch, Southern Utah.

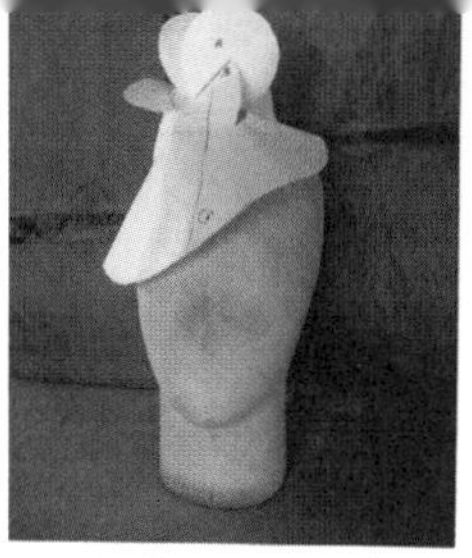
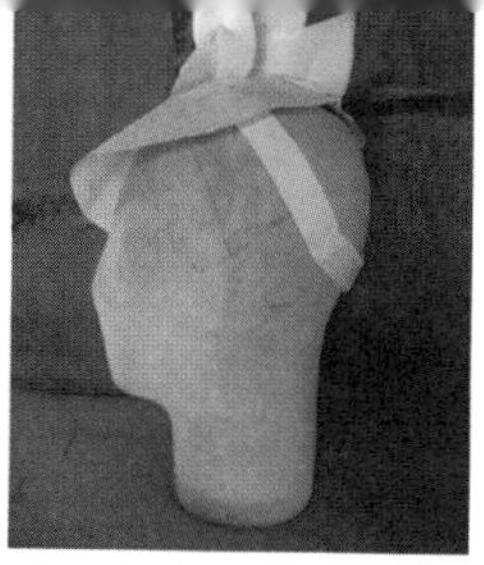

17 APR 2007

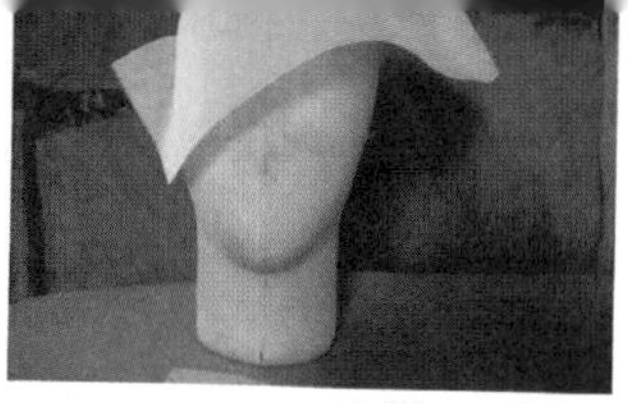

1? APR 2007

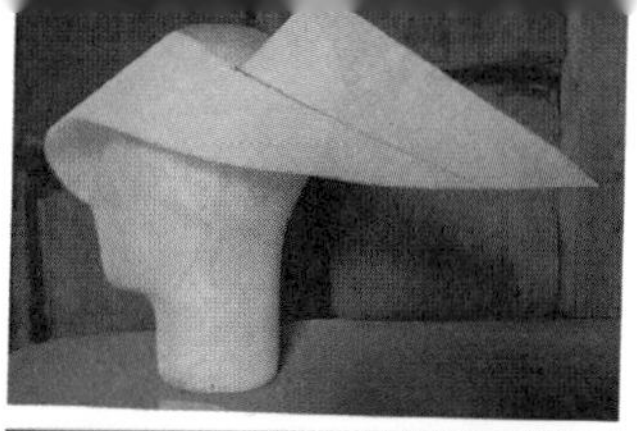
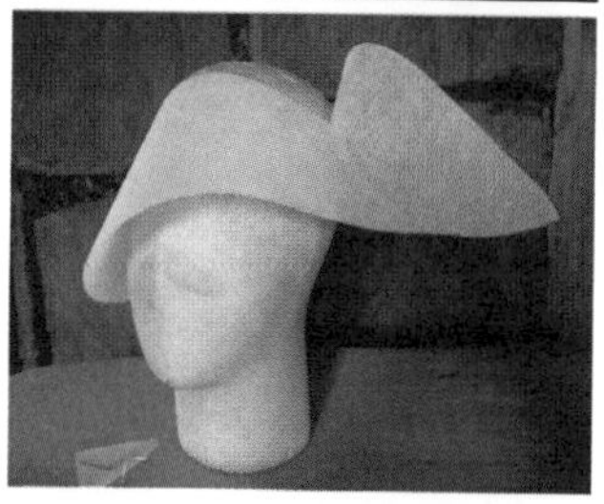
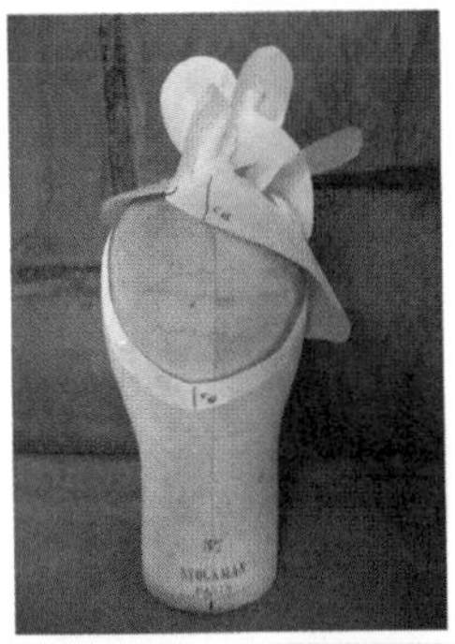

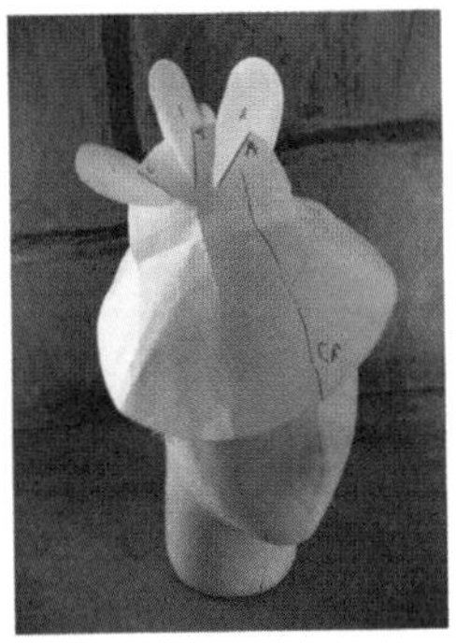

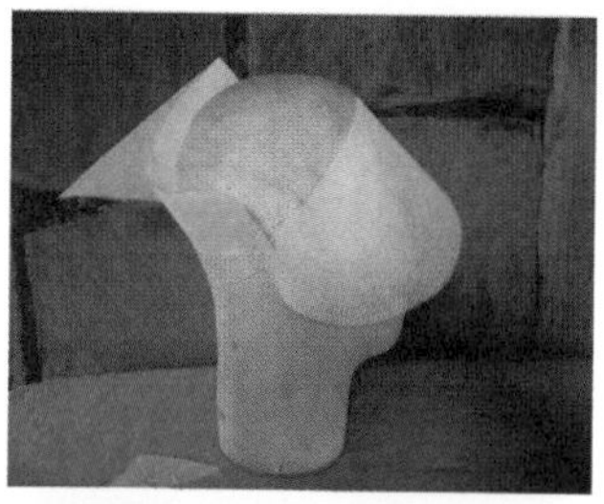

mix beige
(8)
white

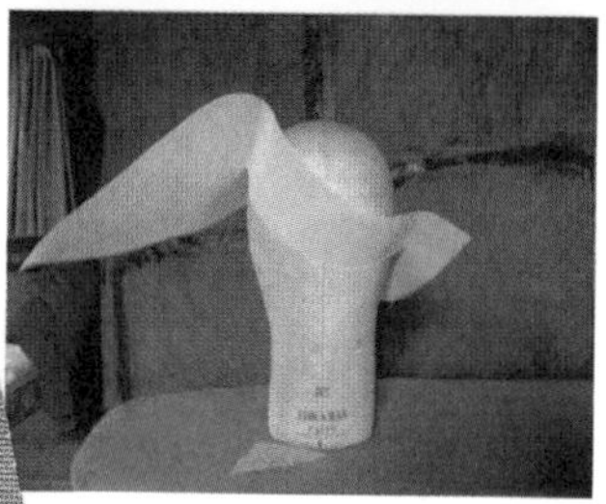

Deborah. Strata. (7)

Earth Deborah. (12)

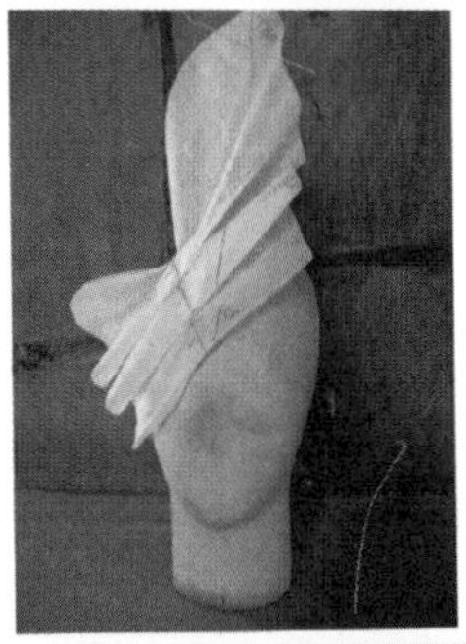

16 APR 2007

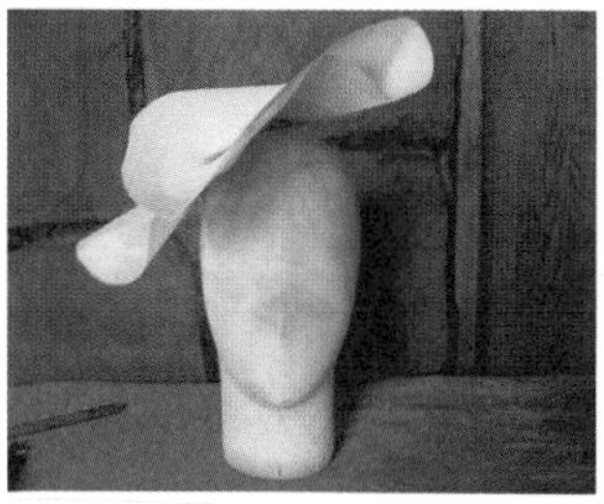

18 APR 2007

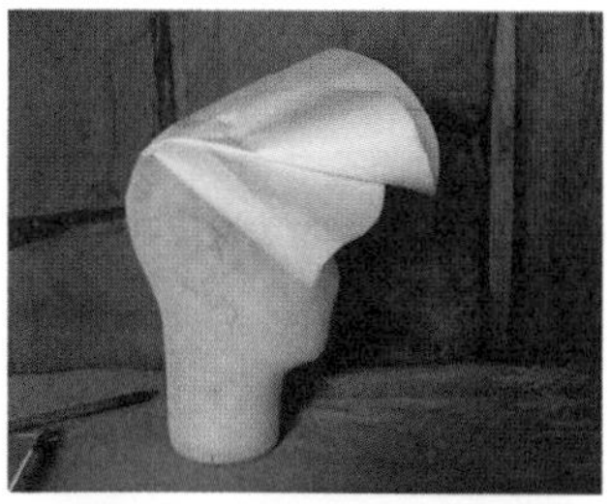
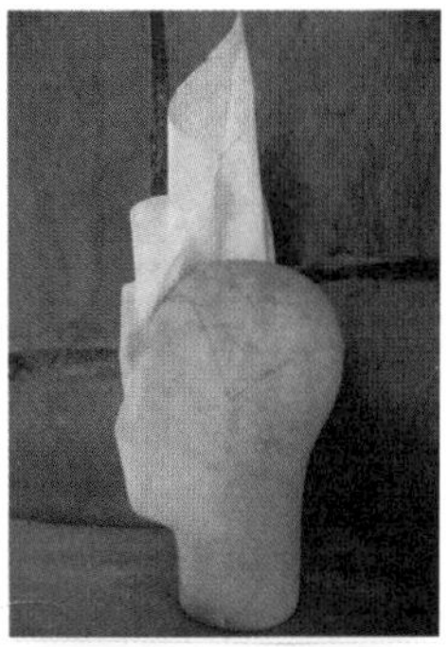
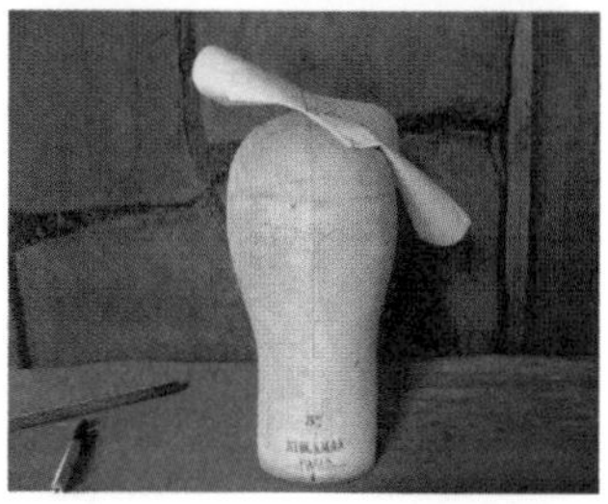

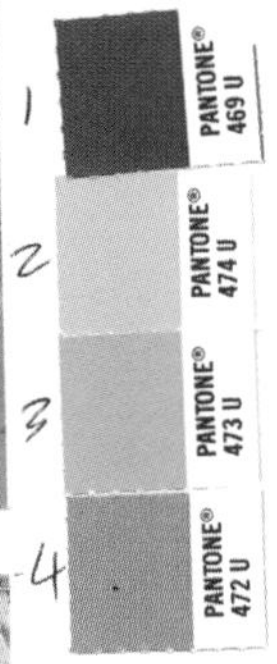

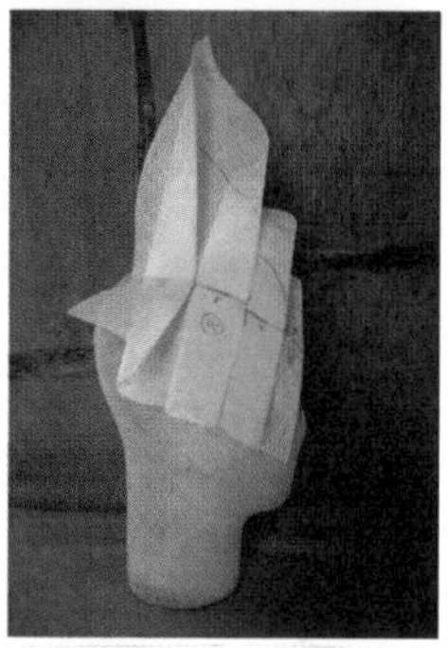

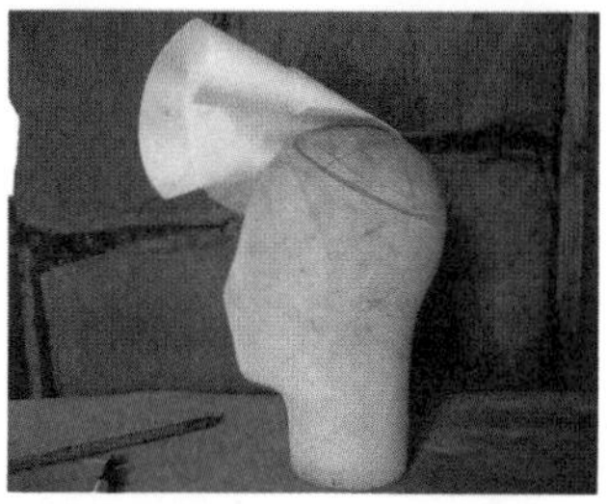
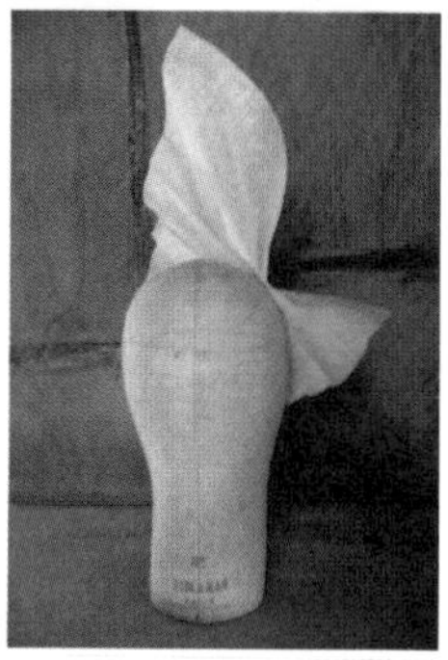

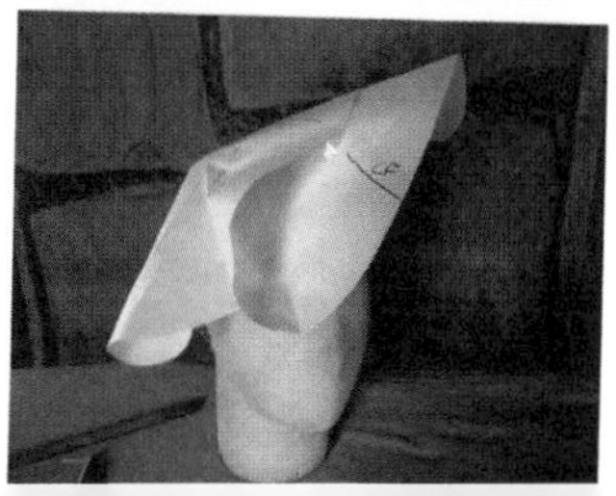

Pale.

degrage brown
terracotta
beige satin
sky blue satin
browns
+ blue

dark.

Stitched + bind.
Small size section crow

'A renowned fashion designer, she left it all behind to live in a leper colony'

HATS OFF TO THE LADY Above: Simonetta Colonna di Cesaro, May 1952. Below: Stephen Jones

My style icon

Milliner **Stephen Jones** pays tribute to Italian fashion diva, Simonetta Colonna di Cesaro

The extraordinary Italian fashion designer Duchess Simonetta Colonna di Cesaro first entered my consciousness in 1976. I was a student at St Martins School of Art when I marvelled over her portrait in a fashion tome. She and her glossy world seemed so urbane, glamorous and exotic – the opposite of the punk sensibility I was surrounded by.

Some 28 years later, I found myself in her apartment in Paris, wondering if she would be the same glamorous diva as the one I had seen in the picture. When I was taken to the drawing room, I was left in no doubt. She detailed her life of '*avventura e pericolo*' in Rome, Paris and India. I discovered her remarkable history: how her family was imprisoned by Mussolini for holding anti-fascist views; how she became a renowned fashion designer; and why she left it all behind to follow her guru to India in 1969, living in a leper colony for 30 years.

I based my last collection on her; although Simonetta wasn't fanatical about hats herself, her archives were full of them. I imagined her wearing my designs, and the collection grew to 21 'haute mode' hats, and Miss Jones and JonesBoy styles. The final stitch went in at 2am on 15 February 2004. It was shown later that day in London, but in my mind it was presented to Simonetta and left in her boudoir for her to contemplate. □

Stephen Jones was talking to Camilla Morton.

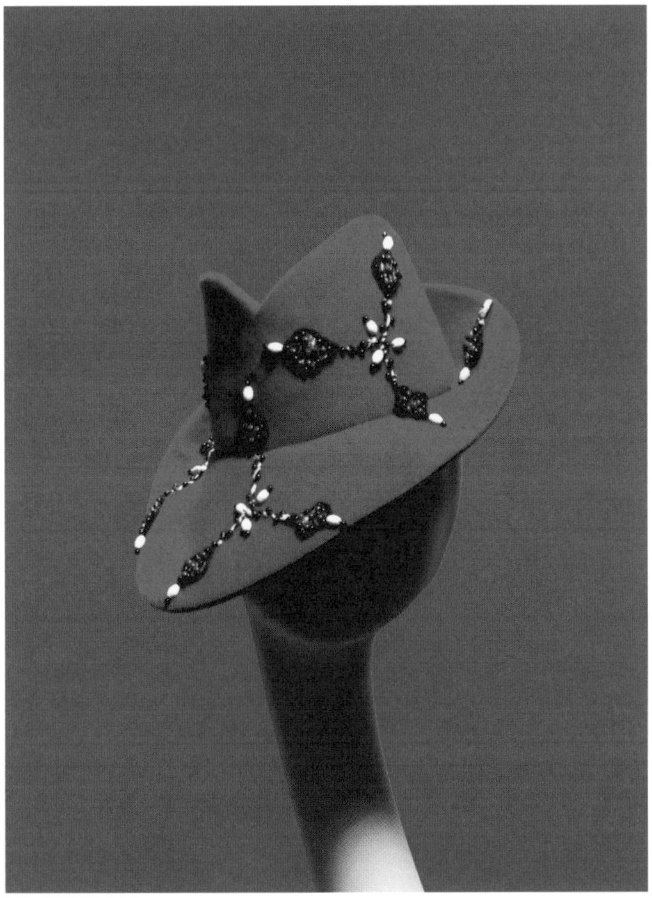

Top left: *Excitement*, A/W 2004–05 collection *La Prima Donna*.
This fedora recalls the silhouette, colour & embroidery in Parkinson's seminal 1959 *Vogue* portrait of Simonetta taken in New York.

Top right: *Coquette*, A/W 2004–05 collection *La Prima Donna*.
Velvet and coq feathers with a rose diamond and ruby pin.

Left: Article on Simonetta Colonna di Cesaro,
Harpers & Queen, September 2004.

book titles represented in his library. That there is something very simple about it, and that Jones believes it all has to do with translation. That you can take a phone (as he did when we sat together) and put it on your head (as he also did) and it becomes a hat. It is a profound point about millinery: that whatever you put on your head becomes a hat despite any previous connotations or alternative uses. Schiaparelli taught us this and Jones uses it to create a lightness of gesture. Sometimes you need to do the literal thing.

A few years ago, I was looking at Jones's *La Prima Donna* collection a lot and ended up incorporating it into an exhibition at Palazzo Pitti, in Florence, which I curated with Maria Luisa Frisa and Vittoria Caratozzolo. The exhibition looked at Simonetta's life as designer and muse, and Jones's collection acted as both a chronological coda to the exhibition and its epigram, embedded as it was within the title of the exhibition — *Simonetta: La Prima Donna della Moda Italiana*. Jones had already translated the duchesa for contemporary eyes in his 2004 collection: one of his trilbies featured embroidery copied from a jacket that she had worn in a famous Norman Parkinson photograph taken at the New York Plaza Hotel in 1949. All of the other pieces in the collection required a very, very keen eye to spot the references to Simonetta, except for this trilby, which came out and declared its purpose. The embroidery was an anachronism on a contemporary hat and it needed to be literal, it needed to be an exact recreation in order to work.

Jones gets nervous about the pedestrian use of such words as anachronistic and futuristic because they are so commonly thrown at hats. He wonders about what is new and what is old, and if we could find a more sophisticated way of describing that relationship. There is an authenticity issue and a descriptive issue, and Jones himself plays with both. His references are so specific — not in a 'this refers to 16th-century lace' kind of way (as Stephen Jones and I discussed) but as links to specific books — it could be 'this piece of lace on this page photographed in black and white with a weird decorative border around the page'. With Jones's collections it is never about a straightforward narrative so recognizing his many references can be difficult. He lets the viewer off the hook, however, by adding a sense of populist ease, he ironizes his research in collection titles and giving wonderfully witty names to his hats (noted on swing tags), which ascribe to each one an imaginary character or an object that the wearer can metamorphose into.

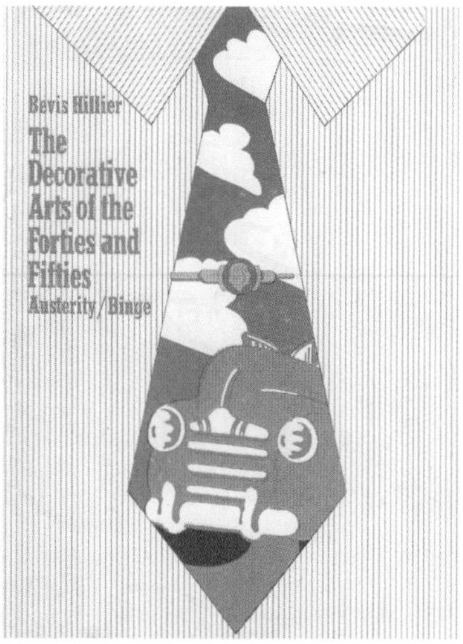

Bevis Hillier, *The Decorative Arts of the Forties and Fifties: Austerity/Binge*, C.N. Potter, New York, 1975.

BIBLIOGRAPHY

Vita Sackville-West, *In Your Garden*, Michael Joseph Ltd, London, 1951.
Fleur Cowles, *The Best of Flair* (1999), Rizzoli Publishers, New York.
A Plethora of Polyhedra in Origami, John Montroll, Antroll Publishing Company, Dover, 2002. Second edition.
Mark Holburn, *Irving Penn regards the Work of Issey Miyake*, First edition, United States Edition, Bulfinch, Boston, 1999. 160 pp.
Joyce Rogers *Flower Arranging*, 1963. First edition.
Eric Kenneway, *Complete Origami*, 1987. Fourth edition.
Norman De Kalb Edwards, *The Art of Flower Arranging*, 1961. Sixth edition.
Alison Brackenbury, *Singing in the Dark*, 2008. First paperback edition.
American Fashion, edited by Sarah Tomerlin Lee for The Fashion Institute, 1975. Seventh edition.
Bevis Hillier, *The Decorative Arts of the Forties and Fifties: Austerity/Binge*, 1975. Seventh edition.
Julia Clements, *Party Pieces – New Ideas for Flower Arranging and Entertaining*, 1960. First edition.

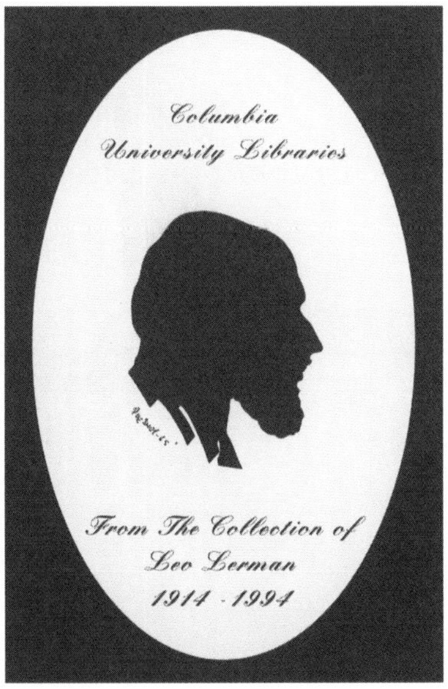

Top: Ex libris in the inside cover of *Party Pieces* by Julia Clements.

Bottom: Julia Clements, *Party Pieces – New ideas for Flower Arranging and Entertaining*, Pearson, London, 1960.

2. Anna Piaggi and the late Vern Lambert were Jones's friends. Lambert, an Australian dress historian and collector of vintage dress, hugely influenced Piaggi's eccentric style. He also worked on *Fashion: An Anthology by Cecil Beaton* in 1971. Anna Piaggi, a stylist and journalist for *Vogue Italia*, is one of Jones's most high profile clients.

'… & then you find it here'

I wanted to know about the 1950s as this period seems to link so many of the books in Jones's library, either by subject, binding or font. It appeared in anthologies on style, film, costume, the art of shop display and Hollywood glamour. Jones was only a child in the 1950s and so the decade belongs to his parents' generation rather than his own; nonetheless, there is a sense of familiarity about the received wisdom of taste and etiquette. It also comes down to one particular book, which he showed me:

'I had this book by Bevis Hillier called *The Decorative Arts of the Forties and Fifties. Austerity/Binge*. This is the second [edition]. This is 1975, but I bought this later; I can't remember. This book influenced me – 1940s, and the war, and then suddenly the 1950s and a Duggie Fields painting. It was great, the graphics around the edge, the writing. I actually have *Party Pieces* by Julia Clements. Duggie Fields I know. [leafing through] I bought this copy about five or six years ago – I found it on the internet. I opened it up and I couldn't believe the ex libris in the inside cover; it had belonged to Leo Lerman. I knew him – he was an art dealer and the art critic of *The New York Times* in the 1950s and 1960s. I actually met him in Venice. I had met him with Evelyn Lambert [the art collector]. I had been to stay with her and did a collection based on her house in the Veneto and I had met him and he was one of the most fascinating people I have ever met in my life – [a] really extraordinary person. I knew when I bought this book that in it was a painting by Duggie Fields, [that] there were other things … which were great [leafing through]. Amazing, amazing … let me just show you. Gypsies – it is so well done … and can I find a 'courtesy of'? Here it is: 'these were from the collection of Vern Lambert' and that octopus earring is on Anna Piaggi's ear. Hillier was a great friend of Vern Lambert's but I didn't find that out until more recently. That tray with the mermaid on it – she [Anna Piaggi] has got it on her desk![2]

It is as though this book managed in some magical way to authenticate all Jones's assumptions – about who was interesting, who met whom, who collected what with whom – and that somehow he is at the interstices of all these connections. It is as though this book is an intensified embodiment of the findings he makes when researching and preparing for his individual collections. Emblematic of how Stephen Jones works, everything comes together.

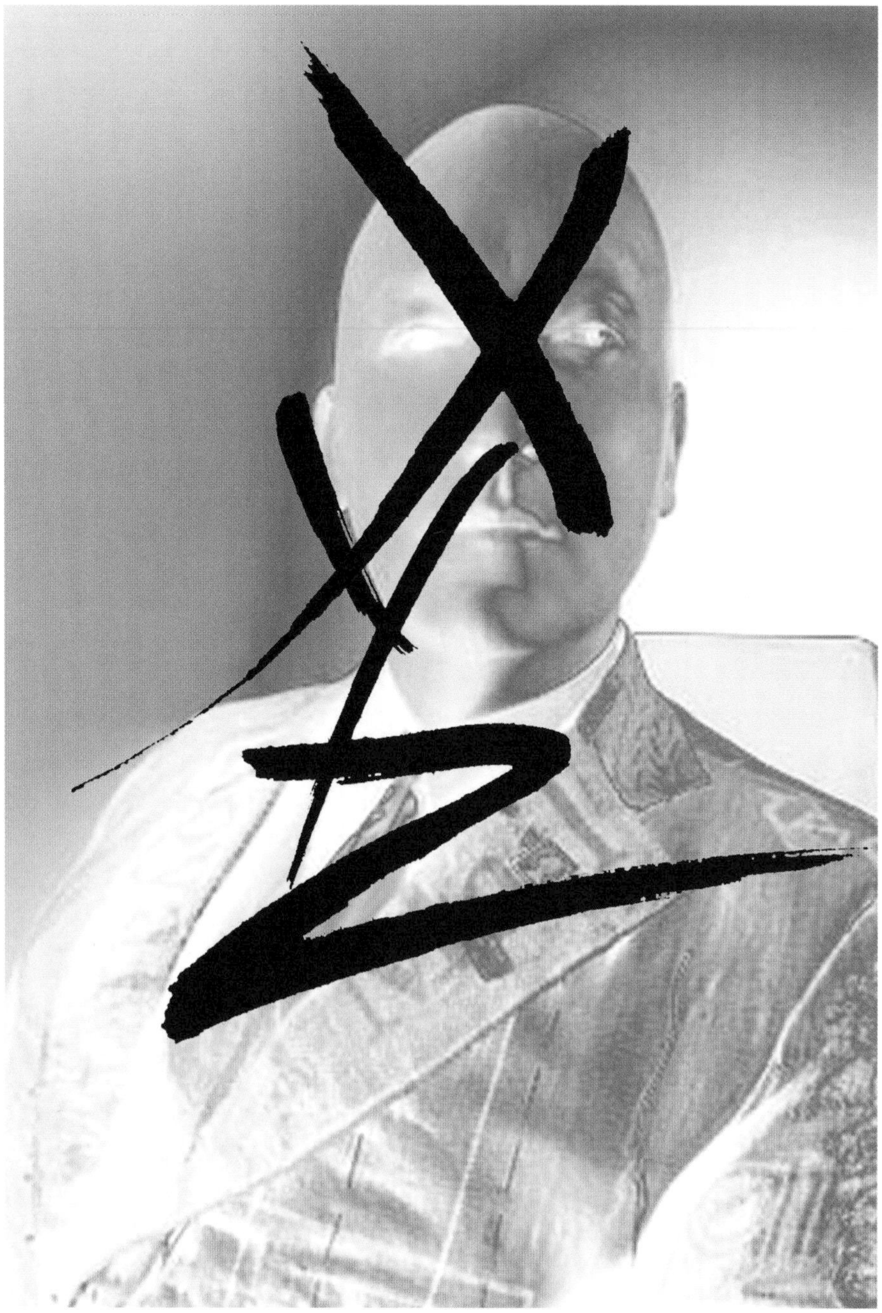

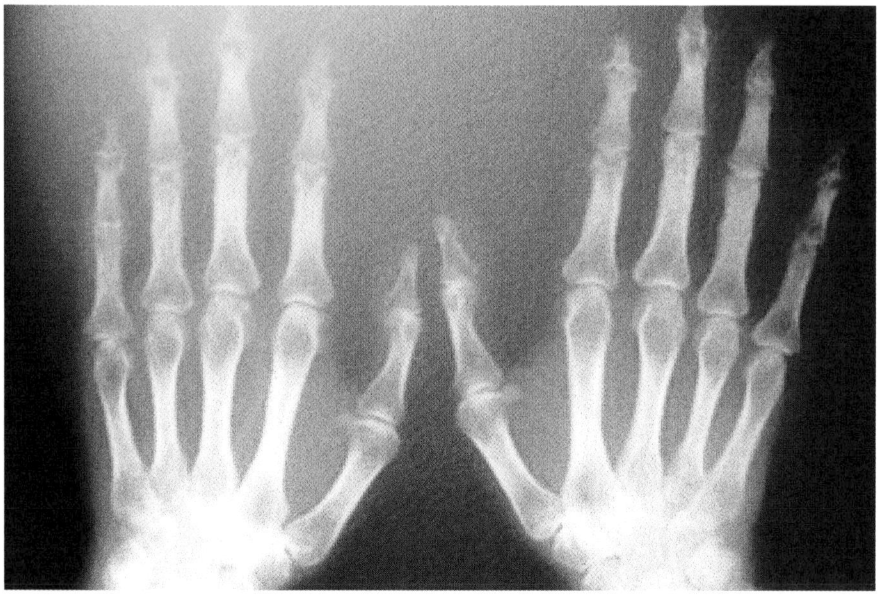

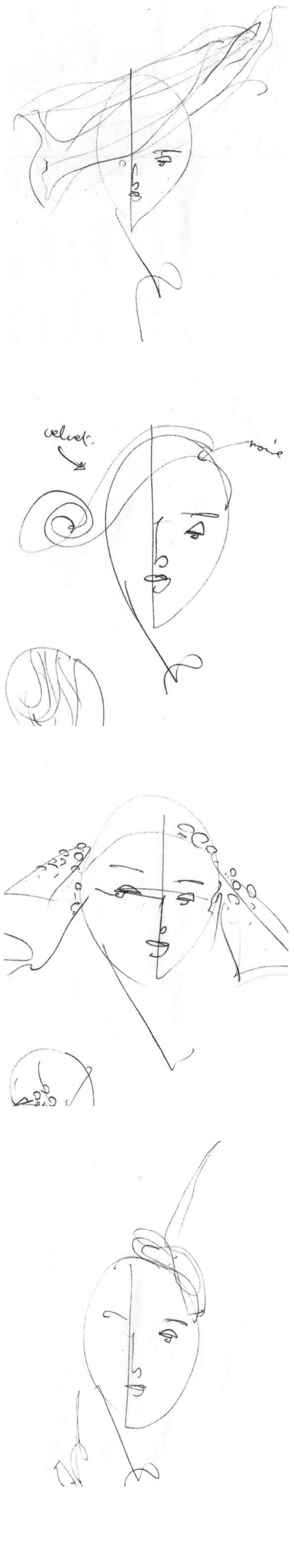

Inspirations and sketches for the A/W 2010–11 collection *XYZ*.

Torso.
photoprint
Sculpture:
all bugles.?

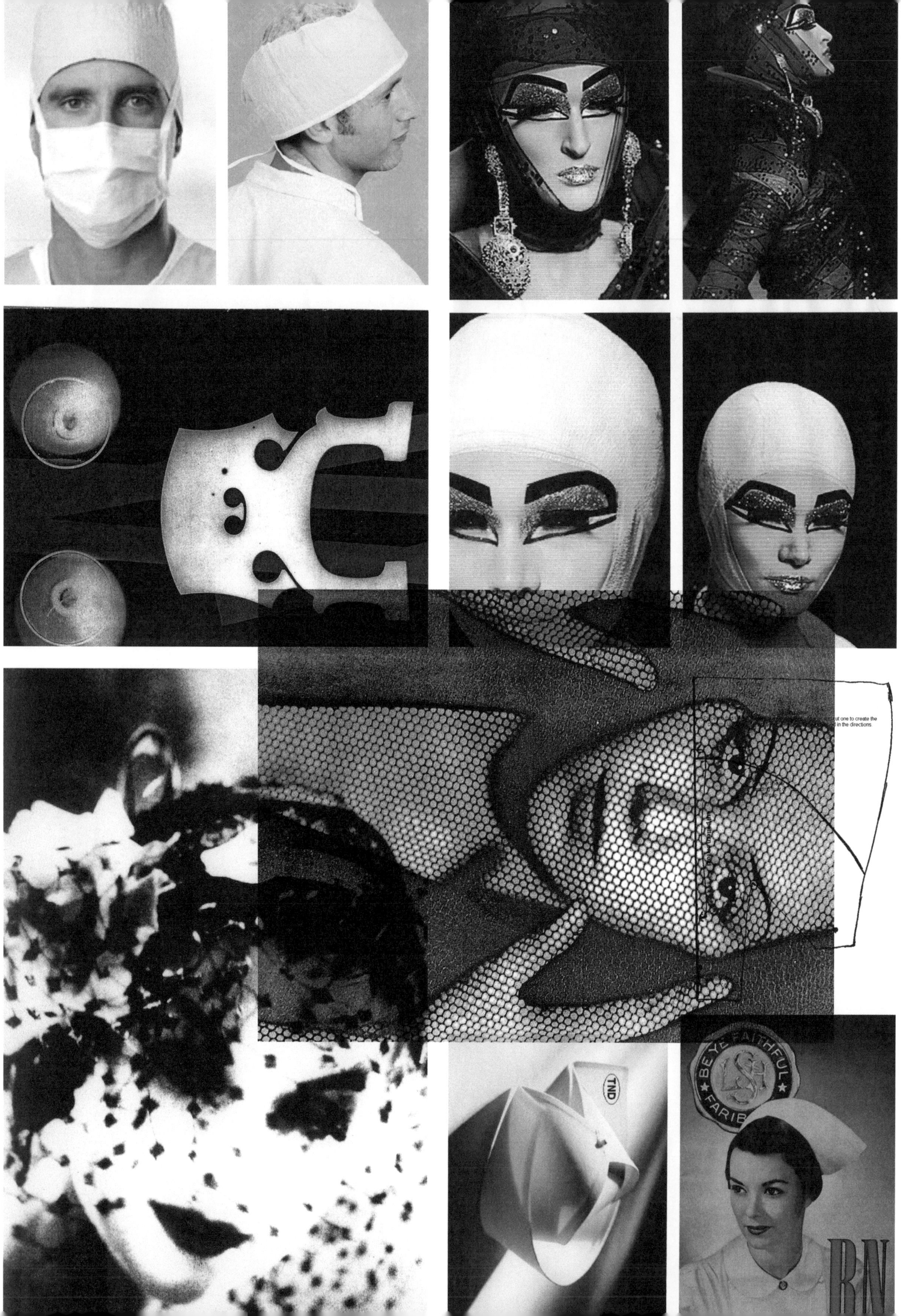
TND
RN

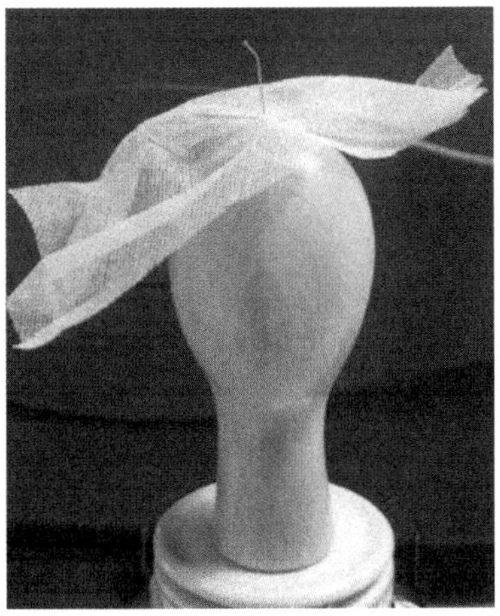
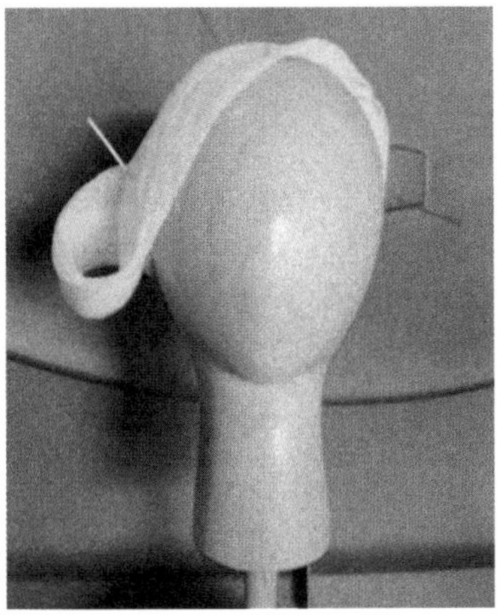
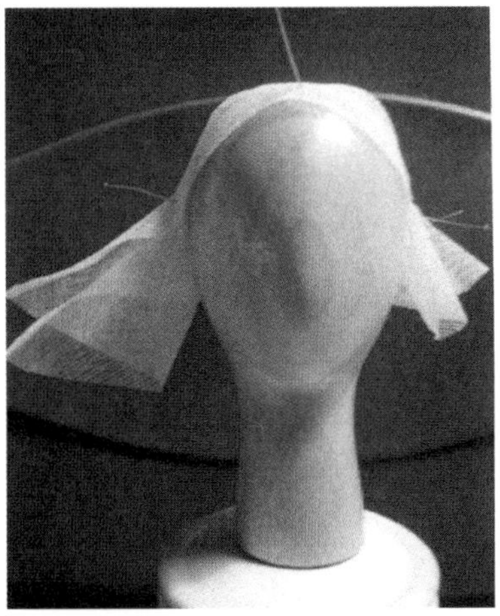
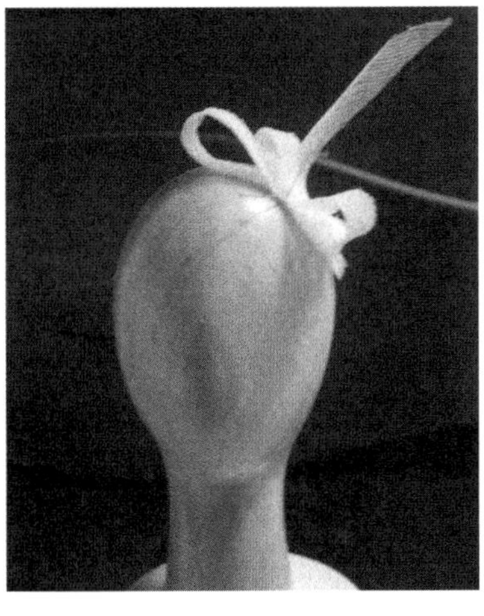

Inspirations, *toiles* and publicity photographs for the A/W 2010–11 collection *XYZ*.
Top: *Bang!*, exploded hat. X-ray brim, pointille crown, taffeta bow, pearl hat pin.
Below: *Triple Vision*, tulle, net and chrome nesting top hats.

Drawing by John Galliano, handsigned, 2010

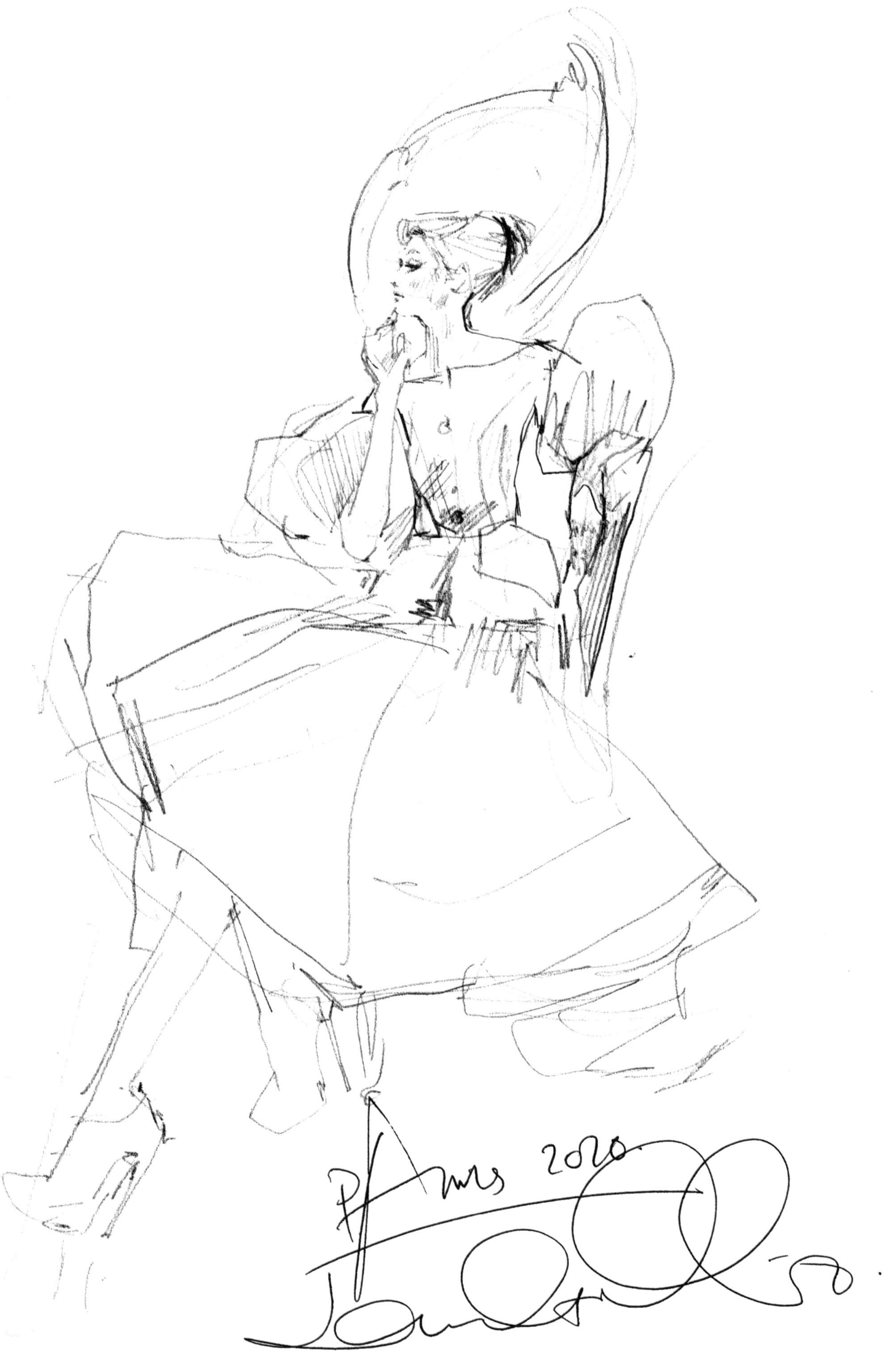
Paris 2020.

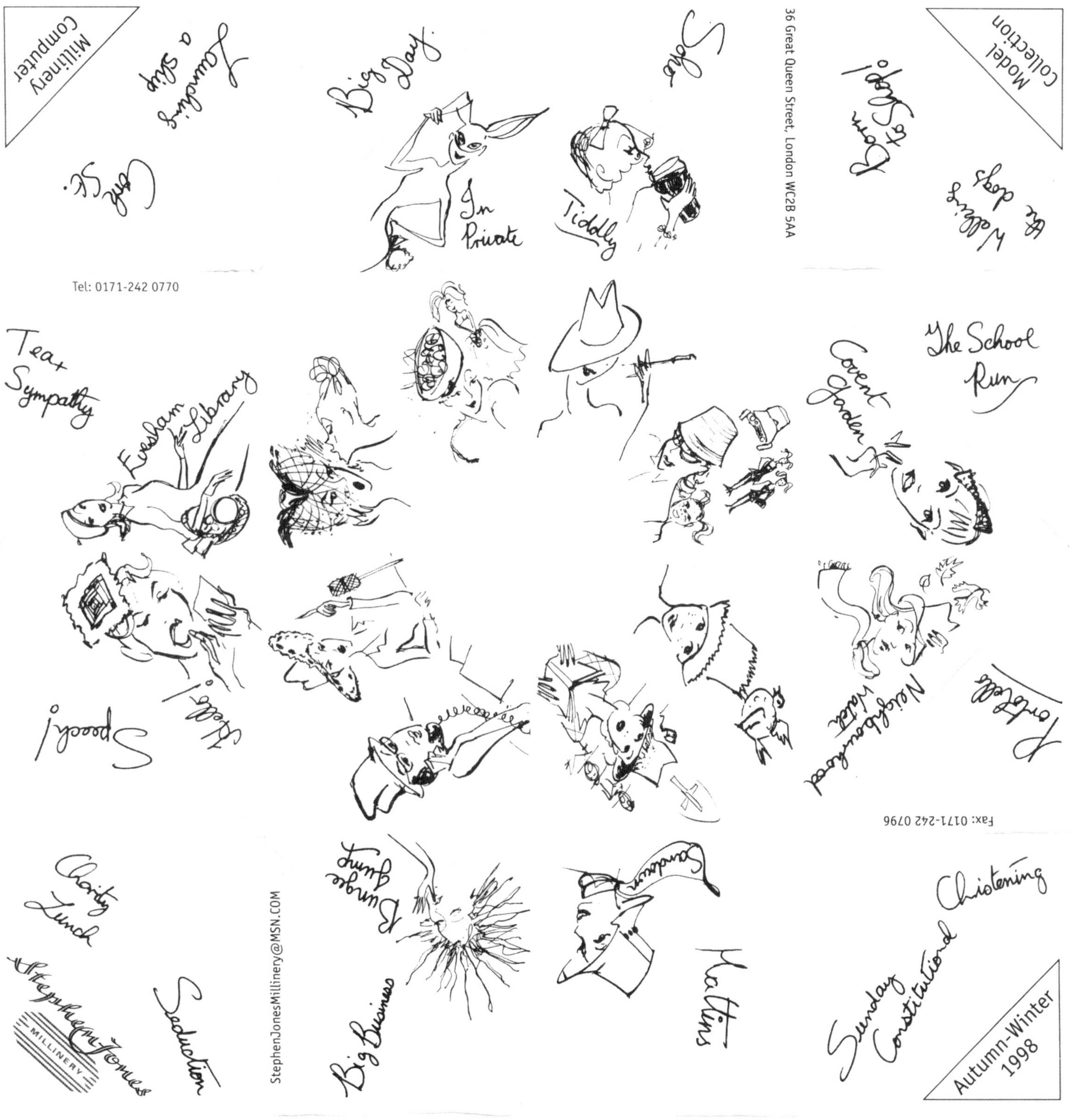

Invitation for A/W 1998–99 collection *Millinery Computer.*

Invitation for first shop opening 1st October 1980.

BIOGRAPHY

Abridged. For further details please go to *www.StephenJonesMillinery.com*

Stephen Jones was born in West Kirby, Cheshire in 1957 and boarded at Liverpool College from 1968. In 1975, he entered High Wycombe College as an art foundation student, and in 1976 attended Saint Martin's School of Art.

1979
Fashion collaboration: Designed Hat Collection for Fiorucci.
Commissions: *Aladdin*, 'Theatre Royal' Windsor.
Awards: B.A. (hons.) in Fashion Design from St Martin's School of Art.

1980
A/W collection: *First Collection.*
Opened first Hat Salon in Endell St, Covent Garden on 1st October.
Music: Visage, Spandau Ballet.

1981
Fashion collaboration: Fiona Dealey
Music: Visage.
Commission: designed Bianca McAlpine's costume for Andrew Logan's 'Alternative Miss World'.

1982
S/S collection: *The Hanging Gardens of Babylon.*
Fashion collaborations: Jasper Conran, Zandra Rhodes.
Film: Appearance in Culture Club video 'Do You Really Want to Hurt Me?'
Music: Culture Club,.
First magazine cover *Tatler* (December).
Shows: Fashion Show for TV programme; BBC's *Riverside*;
Group Fashion Show at 'Le Palace', Paris, hosted by Steve Strange.

1983
S/S collection: *UK/US.*
Fashion collaborations: Jasper Conran, Zandra Rhodes; Designed collection of dresses for 'Suzanne Bartsch' Shop, N.Y.C; Designed fur coat collection for Feldman Furs, N.Y.C.
Music: Spandau Ballet, Grace Jones.
Commissions: *Observer*, Liquifruta.

Invitation for A/W 1985–86 collection *For the Heart of Woman and the Soul of Man*. Models Baillie Walsh & Princess Julia.

1984
S/S collection: *Car Sculpture.*
A/W collection: *Tales of the Alhambra.*
Fashion collaborations: Jasper Conran, Jean Paul Gaultier, Thierry Mugler, Zandra Rhodes.
Commissions: Sold to First Department Store, Bloomingdales, N.Y.C.
Exhibition: Invited to Japan by Isetan Department Store for S.J. Exhibition.
Show: Invited by the Fashion Foundation in Japan for *London Goes to Tokyo* Fashion Show.
Moved to Lexington Street Studio.

1985
A/W collection: *For the Heart of Woman and the Soul of Man.*
S/S collection: *Grand Tour.*
Fashion collaborations: Comme des Garçons, Jasper Conran, Jean Paul Gaultier, Thierry Mugler, Rifat Ozbek.
Film: *Another Country.*
Commissions: Batiste, Schwarzkopf; Ceramics project for Crystal Tiles.
Shows: Invited to Helsinki and Leningrad for British Designer Show;
Invited to New York's Palladium for S.J. show.

1986
A/W collection: *Heads of State.*
S/S collection: *Passport to Pleasure.*
Fashion collaborations: Comme des Garçons, Jasper Conran, Jean Paul Gaultier, Claude Montana, Thierry Mugler.
Film: Hats for Faye Dunaway in *Supergirl*.
Music: Boy George, George Michael, Diana Ross.
Commissions: *Sunday Express*; Sara Lee; Bally; Invited to Japan by the Fashion Foundation, to represent England; Invited to Canada by the International Design Fellowship; Created Hats for 'Régine Chopinot Ballet' with Jean Paul Gaultier; First year to work as Shiseido Consultant.
Exhibitions: Designed Levi Jacket for *Blitz* Magazine; V&A Exhibition, Toulouse, France.

1987
A/W collection: *Stephen Jones World.*
S/S collection: *She.*
Fashion collaborations: Jasper Conran, Enrico Coveri, Claude Montana, Richmond/Cornejo, Vivienne Westwood.
Film: *Beverly Hills Cop II*.
Music: Barbra Streisand, Wet Wet Wet, Wham!.
Commissions: Hats for Pirelli Ballet; Image creator for Shiseido *Integrate* range of cosmetics; Designed shoe collection for Sergio Rossi.
Exhibition: Australian National Gallery starts to collect S.J.

1988
A/W collection: *Room Service.*
S/S collection: *Sunset on Suburbia.*
Fashion collaborations: Enrico Coveri, Katherine Hamnett, Claude Montana, Jil Sander.
Music: Erasure, Bryan Ferry, Madonna.
Commissions: Revlon; Launched Stephen Jones Scarves; Shiseido colour creator.
Exhibitions: *Fashion and Surrealism* Show at F.I.T., N.Y.C. and V&A, London.
Show: Appearance on the *Wogan* Television Show.
Moved to Heddon St.
Geert Bruloot of Louis, Antwerp starts to collect S.J.

1989
A/W collection: *Forty Five Degrees.*
S/S collection: *Ol' Steamy.*
Fashion collaborations: Enrico Coveri, Ghost, Hermès, Claude Montana.
Music: Dead or Alive, The Rolling Stones, Thompson Twins.
Commissions: Twix, Peugeot, Cinzano.

1990
A/W collection: *In Orbit.*
S/S collection: *Passion on the Pampas.*
Fashion collaborations: Enrico Coveri, Katherine Hamnett, Lanvin, Claude Montana, Hanae Mori, Vivienne Westwood.
Music: Paula Abdul, Erasure, Monie Love, Madonna.
Commission: License in Japan for S.J. Cosmetic Bags, T-shirts, Hair Accessories and Handkerchiefs.
Introduced *Miss Jones* Diffusion Hat Range.

1991
A/W collection: *Glamé.*
S/S collection: *Shriek with Chic.*
Fashion collaborations: Katherine Hamnett, Lanvin, Claude Montana, Hanae Mori.
Music: The Rolling Stones.
Commissions: Appointed Shiseido Senior Colour Consultant; Designed an Interior of the Decoration and Design Building, London; Guest make-up artist for the Cover of *Harpers & Queen* (May).
Exhibition: Pitti Trend Gallery, Florence; *Hats* in the Museum of Costume, Bath, England.

Invitation for S/S 1986 collection *Passport to Pleasure*. Model Sibylle de St Phalle.

Invitation for S/S 1991 collection *Shriek with Chic.*

Invitation for A/W 1992–93 collection *Norma Desmond Lives*. Model Gitte Meldgaard.

Invitation for A/W 1997–98 collection *Murder by Millinery*. Illustrations by Robyn Neild.

1992
A/W collection: *Norma Desmond Lives.*
S/S collection: *The Devil is a Woman.*
Fashion collaborations: Katherine Hamnett, Lanvin, Claude Montana, Hanae Mori, André Walker.
Film: *Heirs and Graces.*
Music: Access, U2, Vanessa Williams.
Commissions: Conceptualised four Shiseido Fragrances; Jonathan Ross; Sugar Puffs; Charnos with L'Wren Scott; Worked on Interior Decoration of Sao Schlumberger's apartment in Paris.
Exhibition: The Australian National Gallery, Canberra.

1993
A/W collection: *Xanadu.*
S/S collection: *Souvenirs.*
Fashion collaborations: Balenciaga, BOY, John Galliano, Ghost, Katherine Hamnett, Nicholas Knightly, Claude Montana, John Richmond.
Music: Capella, New Order, U2.
Commissions: Ambre Solaire; Nissan; Fiat; Ford; National Panasonic; Concept and packaging of *Vivace* Fragrance by Shiseido.
Exhibition: *Ahead of Fashion: Hats of the 20th Century*, Philadelphia Museum of Art; *Mad Hatters* Australian National Gallery.
Show: Fashion Show in Belfast.
Launched *JonesGirl* Hats and *Stephen Jones Gloves* in Japan.

1994
A/W collection: *Rococo Futura.*
S/S collection: *Miss World.*
Fashion collaborations: Balenciaga, Vanessa Bruno, John Galliano, Nicholas Knightly, Guy Laroche, Claude Montana.
Commissions: *L'Air du Temps* by Nina Ricci; Moschino.
Exhibition: One Man Exhibition *Rococo Future* at the Ginza Art Space, Tokyo.

1995
A/W collection: *Les Girls.*
S/S collection: *Legasty.*
Fashion collaborations: Balenciaga, John Galliano, Ghost, Guy Laroche, Claude Montana, Rochas, Edina Ronay, Helen Storey.
Music: Marc Almond, Madonna, Billy Ray Martin.
Commissions: Perrier; Chiquita; Yardley; Cellnet.
Award: Nominated as British Accessory Designer of the Year.
Exhibitions: Kyoto Museum of Costume in Japan; National Museum of Ireland.
Opened Shop and Showroom in Covent Garden.

1996
A/W collection: *Contours.*
S/S collection: *Untitled 96.*
Fashion collaborations: Balenciaga, John Galliano, Givenchy, Guy Laroche, Claude Montana, Rochas.
Film: Disney's *101 Dalmatians*.
Music: Belinda Carlisle, Madonna, Mike & the Mechanics, Billy Ray Martin, Take That!, U2.
Commissions: Nicole Kidman;Virgin Airlines; Martini; Martini Rosso.
Awards: Nominated as British Accessory Designer of the Year.
Exhibition: *Stephen Jones* at Isetan Department Store, Tokyo.

1997
A/W collection: *Murder by Millinery.*
S/S collection: *Lotus Eaters.*
Fashion collaborations: Antonio Berardi, Christian Dior, John Galliano, Givenchy, Katherine Hamnett, Holland & Holland, Claude Montana, Emanuel Ungaro, Dirk Van Saene, W&LT.
Films: *Spice World*, *Lost in Space*, *Jurassic Park*.
Music: Madonna, Skunk Anansie, U2.

Exhibition: *The Cutting Edge*, V&A, London.
Commissions: 'Première Vision' with W< *Sunday Telegraph*; Tango; Barclays Bank; Easter Parade Windows for Saks 5th Avenue, N.Y.C.

1998
A/W collection: *Millinery Computer.*
S/S collection: *E=mc²*.
Fashion collaborations: Antonio Berardi, Christian Dior, John Galliano, Keita Maruyama, Claude Montana, Emanuel Ungaro, Matthew Williamson, W&LT.
Film: *Bewitched*; *Entrapment* (20th Century Fox).
Music: Bette Midler, Kylie Minogue.
Exhibitions: *Satellites of Fashion*, Crafts Council, London; *Addressing the Century*, Hayward Gallery, London; *Art Fashion*, Museum of Modern Art San Francisco.
Commissions: Burberry; 'S' brand colour creator, Shiseido; Art Directed Fashion Editorial for *Hanatsubaki* magazine; Easter Parade Windows for Saks 5th Avenue, N.Y.C.
Shows: Fashion Shows in New York, Montreal, and Tokyo.

Invitation for S/S 1999 collection *Pic'n'Mix*.

1999
A/W collection: *Celebration!*
S/S collection: *Pic'n'Mix.*
Fashion collaborations: Antonio Berardi, Burberry, Christian Dior, John Galliano, Holland & Holland, Keita Maruyama, Claude Montana, Emanuel Ungaro, Walter Van Beirendonck, Dries Van Noten.
Film: *A Bug's Life* (Pixar).
Music: All Saints, Celine Dion.
Exhibitions: Hat for U2' Bono in *Rock Style* Exhibition, Metropolitan Museum of Art, N.Y.C; *Addressing the Century*, Hamburg.
Commissions: Parfums Christian Dior; Uniform hats for The British School in Tokyo; Created Anniversary Fragrance for Chacott Ballet Costumes; Easter Parade Windows for Saks 5th Avenue, N.Y.C.; Colour creator for FSP brand, Shiseido.

2000
A/W collection: *Blah Blah Blah.*
S/S collection: *Nursery.*
Fashion collaborations: Antonio Berardi, Christian Dior, John Galliano, Holland & Holland, Jeremy Scott, Emanuel Ungaro, Walter Van Beirendonck.
Music: Kylie Minogue, Spice Girls.
Commissions: Stephen Jones Hat as poster on the Paris Metro.
Exhibitions: 'Les Eccentriques' Show at Printemps, Paris; Union Jack Bowler donated to the Museum of London.

2001
A/W collection: *Queens.*
S/S collection: *Icon.*
Fashion collaborations: Antonio Berardi, Christian Dior, John Galliano, Julien Macdonald, Keita Maruyama, Jil Sander, Jeremy Scott, Emanuel Ungaro, Dries Van Noten, Dirk Van Saene.
Music: Björk, Sophie Ellis-Bextor, Macy Gray, Hear'say, Marleen, Kylie Minogue, Robbie Williams.
Commissions: Stephen Jones Postage Stamp for The Royal Mail; Created *Modem* guide for the Paris Collections with Anna Piaggi; Heals; Esso.
Exhibitions: Crafts Council Exhibition in the Caribbean Contemporary Arts Centre, Trinidad; Museo Del Vestuario, Caracas; Exhibited hats at the *British Fashion* Exhibition, at the Fashion Institute of Technology, N.Y.C; Exhibition of hat photographs in Le Musée des Arts Décoratifs, Paris; Exhibition of summer hats in the costume court of the V&A, London.
Lecture with Anna Piaggi delivered at the Musée de La Mode, Le Louvre, Paris.
Interview with Mr Pearl for the catalogue of *Mutilate?* exhibition 'Mode 2001 Landed' in Antwerp, Belgium.
Show: *Stephen Jones Black* Fashion Show in Moscow, sponsored by *Russian Vogue*.

Invitation for A/W 2001–02 collection *Queens*.

Invitation for A/W 2003–02 collection *Poseur*.

2002
A/W collection: *North.*
S/S collection: *High.*
Fashion collaborations: Antonio Berardi, Christian Dior, John Galliano, Emanuel Ungaro.
Music: Kylie Minogue, Paul Simonon, Steve Strange, Will Young.
Commissions: Agent Provocateur; Top Shop; Lancôme; Rover; Wrote four 'Correspondent' articles for SHOWstudio; Vanity case for Shiseido Hanatsubaki Club.
Exhibitions: Craft Council Exhibition *Satellites of Fashion* continued in Monterrey, Mexico. Tallinn, Estonia, Almaty, Kazakhstan. Krakow, Poland; *Chapeau d'un Jour* and permanent display at the Atelier-Musée du Chapeau in Chazelles, Lyon, France; *Hat & Art* Exhibition in Tilburg, Holland; Ponce sur Loire, France; Louisville, Kentucky; Istanbul, Turkey; Hat in *Men in Skirts* Exhibition, V&A, London; Picture in *L'Enfant Roi,* Paris.
Show: Participated in charity Fashion Shows for Condé Nast, Chicago, *Orange Babies*, Amsterdam and Breast Cancer, London; Bridal Fashion Show in Nagasaki, Japan.

2003
A/W collection: *Poseur.*
S/S collection: *South.*
Fashion collaborations: Hardy Amies, Antonio Berardi, Christian Dior, John Galliano, Ghost, Gibo by Julie Verhoeven, Emanuel Ungaro, Walter Van Beirendonck.
Film: Lady Penelope and Parker in *Thunderbirds*; Created costume and headdress for film for Selfridges *Bodycraze* Exhibition with Walter Van Beirendonck.
Music: Tori Amos, Alison Goldfrapp, P!nk.
Commissions: Top Shop; Dita Von Teese.
Exhibitions: *21st Century Dandy*, British Council Exhibition in Krasnoyarsk, Siberia and Tel Aviv; *Salad Dressing* Exhibition in Copia: The American Centre for Wine, Food & the Arts, California, USA; Contributed to Manolo Blahnik's Exhibition catalogue for the Design Museum, London.
Shows: Bridal Fashion Show in Nagasaki, Japan; Performed in Vienna's *Life Ball* with Anna Piaggi.

2004
A/W collection: *La Prima Donna.*
S/S collection: *Hollywood Regency.*
Fashion collaborations: Azzedine Alaïa, Antonio Berardi, Christian Dior Haute Couture, Prêt-à-Porter, Golf, Ski and Surf Collections, John Galliano, Ghost, Gibo by Julie Verhoeven, Emanuel Ungaro.
Film: Dita Von Teese as Gala Dalí in *The Death of Salvador Dalí* by Delaney Bishop.
Music: Christina Aguilera, Beyoncé for L'Oréal, Kylie Minogue, P!nk, Usher.
Commissions: Hat for British Airways Concorde and Special Promotions; MAC Cosmetics; Shiseido Hanatsubaki; Futsuke.
Awards: Nominated as British Accessory Designer of the Year.
Exhibitions: *The London Look* at Museum of London UK; *21st Century Dandy*, British Council Touring Exhibition, *Hats & Gloves*, City Gallery Leicester; *Body Extensions*, MUDAC, Lausanne; *Excess* at Pitti Foundation, Florence, Italy; *Wild: Fashion Untamed*, The Metropolitan Museum of Art, N.Y.C.
Show: *Stephen Jones Hats* in Dubai, in association with Saks 5th Avenue, N.Y.C.

Invitation for A/W 2005–06 collection *Jubilee*. Illustration by Robyn Neild.

2005
A/W collection: *Jubilee.*
S/S collection: *Handmade in England.*
Quarter Century Anniversary: 25 years since Stephen Jones opened his first Hat Salon in Endell St, Covent Garden.
Fashion collaborations: Basso & Brooke, Antonio Berardi, Comme des Garçons, Giles Deacon, Christian Dior, John Galliano, Ghost, Emanuel Ungaro;
Capsule Collections for Liberty of London and Dover Street Market.
Film: Created *C1/4* in collaboration with Delaney Bishop for SHOWstudio Moving Image.
Music: Millinery and costumes for Kylie Minogue's *Showgirl* tour; Marilyn Manson's *Against All Odds* tour; Mick Jagger for *A Bigger Bang* tour; Róisín Murphy, Usher.
Exhibitions: *C1/4*, Major Retrospective Exhibition held at Dover Street Market in London in conjunction with Rei Kawakubo; Artwork contributed to The Tate Gallery's *40 Artists, Forty Days* Olympic Gallery; Artwork contributed to the *Hitchhiker's Guide to the Galaxy* Exhibition

at the Science Museum, London; Sculpture shown at Peanuts Life Design, Suntory Museum, Tokyo Japan.
Commissions: Immodesty Blaize's show *Burlesque*, London; *Lady Windermere's Fan* at the Gate Theatre, Dublin; MAC; Pirelli Calendar; MAC Cosmetics in Shanghai; Created fragrance *Eightieslut* to coincide with *i-D* magazine's 25th Anniversary *i-Dentity* Exhibition at the Fashion & Textiles Museum, London.
Shows: Fashion Show in Colombo, Sri Lanka, in association with London College of Fashion & Moratuwa University; Bridal Fashion Show in Nagasaki, Japan in collaboration with Suehiro.

2006
A/W collection: *Timetravel.*
S/S collection: *Travelogue.*
Fashion collaborations: Hardy Amies, Antonio Berardi, Hussein Chalayan, Comme des Garçons, Jasper Conran, Giles Deacon, Christian Dior, John Galliano, Marc Jacobs, Julien Macdonald, Keita Maruyama, Giambattista Valli; Capsule Collections for Liberty of London, Colette (Paris, France) *UK JACK OK!*, Isetan (Tokyo, Japan), 10 Corso Como/Comme des Garçons/Stephen Jones (Milan, Italy).
Film: Cate Blanchett in *The Golden Age*, Keira Knightley in *Atonement*, Virginie Ledoyen.
Music: Millinery and costumes for Kylie Minogue's *Showgirl* tour.
Commissions: MAC; Dita Von Teese; Reindeer pop up restaurant tiara; Launched *Stephen Jones1*, exclusively through Dover Street Market London and Tokyo; Guest Editor of *.Cent* magazine; Art Directed *WinterGarden* beauty shoot for *Hanatsubaki* magazine.
Exhibitions: *C1/4*, 'Stephen Jones Hats fly from London to Tokyo' Exhibition held at 10 Corso Como/Comme des Garçons, Aoyama, Tokyo in conjunction with Rei Kawakubo; *Anglomania*, Metropolitan Museum of Art, N.Y.C.; Anna Piaggi's *Fashionology* Exhibition at the V&A, London; Series of designer portraits with Hats for Canon/Red Cross *The Other Side of Fashion* Exhibition (London/Paris/Milan).
Shows: Fashion Show in London in association with Melbourne Racing Carnival; MAC *Fashion Cares* Aids fundraiser in Toronto; *The Summer Hat Party* at Debenham House London, celebrating 25 years of Summer Hats; Performance as magician with Anna Piaggi onstage at the Olympia, Paris for Jean Paul Gaultier's 30th year Anniversary Party.

2007
A/W collection: *Shangri-La.*
S/S collection: *Artifice.*
Fashion collaborations: Comme des Garçons, Giles Deacon, Christian Dior, John Galliano, Marc Jacobs, L'Wren Scott, Giambattista Valli, Walter Van Beirendonck.
Music: Mick Jagger for *A Bigger Bang* tour; Millinery and costumes for Kylie Minogue's *Showgirl* tour.
Exhibitions: *Orientalism*, FIT, N.Y.C.; *The Golden Age of Couture*, V&A, London; *Blog.mode*, Metropolitan Museum, N.Y.C.; Mini Retrospective at Seibu Shibuya, Tokyo; *Kylie* Exhibition, Melbourne and V&A, London; Evening with curator Oriole Cullen at the V&A *High Fashion Hats*; Masterclass at the Royal Academy of Fine Arts in Antwerp.
Commissions: Anniversary Caperino and Peperone hats for Colette, Paris; Art Directed *Hats and Hair* beauty shoot for *Hanatsubaki* magazine; Gap (Red) project curated by Katie Grand; Opened Stephen Jones/Comme des Garçons shops in Seibu, Shibuya and Matsuya Yurakucho, Tokyo.

2008
A/W collection: *Covent Garden.*
S/S collection: *Desert Rose.*
Fashion collaborations: Comme des Garçons, Giles Deacon, Christian Dior, John Galliano, Marc Jacobs, Loewe, L'Wren Scott, Walter Van Beirendonck.
Film: Directed *Political Fashion* film for SHOWstudio.
Commissions: 'Reinvented' hat for Oxfam; Created jewellery for the V&A Bollinger Jewellery Gallery; Creative direction of Spray de Mode/Bumble&Bumble; Guest appearance as Fashion DJ for SHOWstudio; Headdresses for Ballet Rambert's production of *Eternal Light*; Created ballet with London Contemporary Dance Theatre for British Fashion Awards; Launch of Stephen Jones/Comme des Garçons Fragrance at Dover Street Market.
Awards: Appointed Honorary Professor, University of the Arts, London; Outstanding Achievement in Fashion Design Award, British Fashion Awards.

Invitation for S/S 2006 collection *Timetravel*.

Invitation for A/W 2007–08 collection *Shangri-La*. Illustration by Julie Verhoeven.

Invitation for S/S 2010 collection *ABC*.
Illustration by Paul Simonon.

Exhibitions: *Stephen Jones Peep Show*, Cosmoprof, Bologna; Contributed to *Simonetta, la Prima Donna della Moda Italiana* Exhibition at Pitti Palace, Florence; Commemorative hat for *Carmen Miranda* Exhibition, São Paulo fashion week, Brazil; Hats for *Bill Gibb, a personal Journey*, Museum of Costume, Bath; *Superheroes*, Metropolitan Museum of Art, N.Y.C.; Retrospective Exhibition, On Pedder, Hong Kong.

2009
A/W collection: *Albertopolis.*
S/S collection: *VandA.*
Fashion collaborations: Kinder Aggugini, Comme des Garçons, Giles Deacon, Christian Dior, John Galliano, Marc Jacobs, Donna Karan, Loewe, L'Wren Scott, Walter Van Beirendonck.
Film: Hats for Audrey Tatou in *Coco avant Chanel*; *Hats Off* films on SHOWstudio.
Music: Bryan Adams, Kylie Minogue, Take That!.
Commissions: Dita Von Teese/Crazy Horse; Immodesty Blaize; Perrier Jouët; Printemps; Disneyland Paris.
Awards: Royal Designer for Industry, Royal Society of Arts; Design Star Honoree, Fashion Group International Awards, New York; Outstanding Contribution to Fashion, *Elle* Style Awards; Best Fine Binding, *Hats, an Anthology by Stephen Jones* by Oriole Cullen, British Book Awards.
Exhibitions: *Hats, an Anthology by Stephen Jones*, V&A, London (100,000 visitors); Arnhem Mode Biennale, Holland; Trading Museum, Tokyo.
Shows: *Royal Ascot*; *Fashion Rocks*, Rio; *Vivienne Westwood*, Tokyo; Port Eliot Lit Fest, Cornwall; Curated *Headonism* Group Show and Exhibit of young London milliners to open 25 years of London Fashion Week with Mayor Boris Johnson.

2010
A/W collection: *XYZ.*
S/S collection: *ABC.*
1st October 2010, 30th Year Anniversary of the opening of Stephen Jones Millinery.
Fashion collaborations: Kinder Aggugini, Comme des Garçons, Giles Deacon, Christian Dior, John Galliano, Donna Karan, Loewe, L'Wren Scott, Walter Van Beirendonck; John Galliano Accessories Collection for Men and Women: Hats, Scarves, Gloves, Umbrellas; Capsule Collection for Dorchester Hotels Collection.
Film: *W.E.* directed by Madonna; *Coco avant Chanel* nominated for an Oscar, a César and a BAFTA.
Music: Christina Aguilera, Jamiroquai, Simon Le Bon.
Commissions: Show *Queen Vodka*, Coworth Park Hotel; *Ecococo* environmental magazine; S.J. Design Map, London Design Week, V&A, London.
Award: Order of the British Empire from Her Majesty the Queen.
Exhibitions: *Stephen Jones & the Accent of Fashion*, MoMu Fashion Museum, Antwerp; *The Enchanted Palace*, Kensington Palace, London; *Hats, an Anthology by Stephen Jones* Queensland Art Gallery Brisbane (250,000 visitors); *Travelling Hats*, CDG Trading Museum, Tokyo; *Le chapeau, pas si bête !* at Musée des Chapeaux, Chazelles, France.
Shows: *Royal Ascot* (and appearance in poster); *Fashion Night Out* Show, N.Y.C.

PHOTO CREDITS

P.4 Izima Kaoru; Hair & Make-up: Masa Ohtake
P.6 Nick Knight
P.9 Willy Vanderperre; Styling: Olivier Rizzo
P.10–11 Sølve Sundsbø
P.12 Peter Ashworth
P.14 Top: Peter Ashworth;
Bottom: Courtesy of Stephen Jones Archives
P.15 Illustration by Lee Sheldrick
P.16 Roxanne Lowit
P.17 Top: Peter Ashworth;
Bottom: Courtesy of Stephen Jones Archives
P.18 Top: Patrick Trautwein; Bottom: Mario Testino
P.19 www.justinephotography.com
P.20 Juergen Teller
P.22 Left: Michel Momy;
Right: Courtesy of Stephen Jones Archives
P.23 Paolo Roversi
P.24 Courtesy of Stephen Jones Archives
P.25 © Rex Features Ltd.
P.26 Ben Hassett
P.28–29: Hugo Maertens
P.31 Top: Courtesy of Stephen Jones Archives;
Bottom: Courtesy of Jean Paul Gaultier Archives
P.32 Chris Moore
P.33 Top: Thierry Chomel;
Bottom: Courtesy of *Collezioni* Archives.
P.34 Top: Herb Ritts; Bottom: Ken McKay/
Rex Features Ltd.
P.35 Sandrine Dulermo & Michael Labica –
www.absynthphoto.com
P.36–37 Courtesy of Universal Studios
Licensing LLLP
P.38 Courtesy of Stephen Jones Archives
P.39 David Bailey
P.40 Hugo Maertens
P.41 Courtesy of Stephen Jones Archives
P.42 Top: Robert Doisneau;
Bottom: Christian Dior Archives
P.43 Top: Hugo Maertens;
Bottom: Peter Ashworth
P.44 Peter Ashworth
P.45 Courtesy of Stephen Jones Archives
P.46 Geert Bruloot
P.47 Hugo Maertens
P.48–49 Lesley Robeson
P.50 Karl Lagerfeld
P.51–52 Hugo Maertens
P.53 Courtesy of Stephen Jones Archives
P.54 Hugo Maertens
P.55 www.justinephotography.com
P.56 Gitte Meldgaard;
Art Direction: Robert Sumrell
P.57–58 Hugo Maertens
P.59 Karl Lagerfeld
P.60 Peter Ashworth
P.61 Hugo Maertens
P.62 Steven Meisel
P.63–65 Hugo Maertens
P.66 Courtesy of Stephen Jones Archives
P.67 Hugo Maertens
P.68 Roxanne Lowit
P.69 Courtesy of Stephen Jones Archives
P.70 FoMu Antwerp/Jacques Sonck
P.71 Barry J. Holmes
P.72 YAMA
P.73 Hugo Maertens
P.74 Mario Testino; Styling: Hamish Bowles
P.76 Top: Emma Woolard;
Bottom: Cover Roxy Music: EMI Archives;
Photograpy: Karl Stoecker; Styling: Antony Price
P.77 Courtesy of Stephen Jones Archives;
Styling: Frans Ankoné
P.78 Peter Ashworth
P.79 Robyn Beeche
P.80 Harvey Yamaguchi
P.81 David Bailey
P.82 Top: © Sheila Rock/Rex Features Ltd.;
Bottom: Robyn Beeche
P.83–84 Peter Ashworth
P.85 Top: Derek Ridgers;
Bottom: Courtesy of Stephen Jones Archives
P.86–87 Herbert Schulz
P.88 Harvey Yamaguchi
P.89 Peter Ashworth
P.90 Robyn Beeche
P.91 Peter Lindbergh
P.92 Courtesy of Stephen Jones Archives
P.93 Courtesy of Stephen Jones Archives
P.94 Angelo Pennetta
P.95 Andrew Macpherson/The Rappaport Agency
P.96–105 Bardo Fabiani
P.106 Jean-Baptiste Mondino
P.108 Top: Rex Features Ltd.; Bottom: Chris Moore
P.109 Courtesy of Stephen Jones Archives
P.110–111 Tyen
P.112 Paolo Roversi
P.113 Top: Pascal Therme; Bottom: Susie Taylor
P.114 © Herb Ritts Foundation;
Model: Carolyn Murphy
P.115 Paolo Roversi
P.116 Bardo Fabiani
P.117 Courtesy of Stephen Jones Archives
P.118–120 Etienne Tordoir
P.121 Paolo Roversi
P.122 www.justinephotography.com
P.123 David Downton
P.124 Mark Segal
P.126 Etienne Tordoir
P.127 Lesley Robeson/
Courtesy of Stephen Jones Archives
P.128 Bardo Fabiani; Model: Lily Cole
P.129 Lauren van der Stockt/
Courtesy of Christian Dior Archives
P.130 Bardo Fabiani
P.131 Hugo Maertens
P.132 Etienne Tordoir
P.133 Mert Alas & Marcus Piggott
P.134 Peter Ashworth
P.135 Courtesy of *Collezioni* Archives
P.136–137 Enrique Badulescu
P.138 Ronald Stoops
P.139 Etienne Tordoir
P.140 Dan Lecca
P.141–143 Ronald Stoops
P.144 David Bailey
P.146 Nick Knight
P.147 Perou/CameraPress
P.148 Rrosemary
P.149 Terence Donovan
P.150 Top: Courtesy of Stephen Jones Archives;
Bottom: Peter Lindbergh
P.151 Peter Ashworth
P.152 Illustration by Barbara Hulanicki
P.153 Top: Finlay Mackay; Bottom: Hugo Maertens
P.154 Peter Ashworth
P.155 Mark C. O'Flaherty
P.156 www.justinephotography.com
P.157 © Suzy Menkes
P.158 © Popperfoto/Getty Images
P.159 Top: Terence Donovan;
Styling: Michael Roberts; Bottom:
Courtesy of Stephen Jones Archives
P.160 Peter Ashworth
P.161 Regan Cameron/Art & Commerce
P.162–164 Hugo Maertens
P.165 Sølve Sundsbø
P.166 Robert Fairer
P.167 Hugo Maertens
P.168–170 Sølve Sundsbø
P.172–173 Annie Leibovitz/Contact Press Images;
Courtesy of the artist
P.174 Kate Garner
P.175 Inez Van Lamsweerde & Vinoodh Matadin
P.177 Angus McBean © Harvard Theatre
Collection, Houghton Library, Harvard University
P.178–179 www.justinephotography.com
P.180 Ben Hassett
P.181 © Charles Sykes/Rex Features Ltd.
P.182 Juergen Teller
P.183 Jason Pietracatella
P.184 Sebastian Faena
P.185 Robyn Beeche
P.186 Sølve Sundsbø
P.187 Top: Mario Testino; Courtesy Emma
Harrison; Bottom: Steven Klein
P.188 Left: Annie Leibovitz at Contact Press;
Right: Mert Alas & Marcus Piggott
P.189 Tim Bret Day
P.190 Paolo Roversi
P.192 Noboru Morikawa
P.193 Chris Nicholls
P.194 Sølve Sundsbø
P.195 François Nars; Make-up: Ayako;
Styling: Patti Wilson
P.196–197 Nick Knight
P.198 Sølve Sundsbø
P.199 Tony Viramontes
P.200 Courtesy of Stephen Jones Archives
P.201 Izima Kaoru; Hair & Make-up: Masa Ohtake
P.202 Paolo Roversi
P.204–205 Courtesy of Stephen Jones Archives
P.206 Courtesy of Stephen Jones Library
P.207 Courtesy of Norton Simon Museum
P.208 Manchester Art Gallery
P.209 Courtesy of Stephen Jones Library
P.210–214 Courtesy of Stephen Jones Archives
P.215 Courtesy of Stephen Jones Library
P.216–217 Courtesy of Stephen Jones Archives
P.218 Norman Parkinson/Fiona Cowan
P.219 Peter Ashworth
P.221 Courtesy of Stephen Jones Library
P.222–225 Courtesy of Stephen Jones Archives
P.227 John Galliano
P.228–235 Courtesy of Stephen Jones Archives

All images taken by Hugo Maertens feature hair styling by Pascal Van Loenhout for Bumble&Bumble.

COLOPHON

EXHIBITION

The exhibition was organised by the Executive Board of the Council of the Province of Antwerp Board Provinciebestuur Antwerpen.

Provincial Governor
Cathy Berx
Provincial Registrar
Danny Toelen
Members of the Executive Board
Ludo Helsen, Rik Röttger, Koen Helsen, Marc Wellens, Inga Verhaert, Bart De Nijn
Head of Cultural Service
Walter Rycquart

Exhibition Design
Geert Bruloot

Curators
Geert Bruloot & Kaat Debo
in collaboration with
Stephen Jones

MoMu

Director
Kaat Debo
Loan Administration
Karen Van Godtsenhoven
Production Manager
Inge Theylaert
Press & Communication
David Flamée, Leen Borgmans
Conservation & Installation Objects
Erwina Sleutel, Kim Verkens, Ellen Machiels, Kenny Damian, Wim Mertens
Education
Frieda De Booser

With special thanks to:

Lesley Robeson, Craig West, Veronique Thomson, Adele Mildred & the team at Stephen Jones Millinery;
Geert Bruloot & Eddy Michiels;
The team at MoMu;
Anna Piaggi, Bardo Fabiani, Luca Stoppini;
Sofie Carré;
Robby Timmermans, Guy Voet, FotoMuseum Provincie Antwerpen;
Production Volunteers: Dimitra Apostolidis, Isa De Wispelaere, Sylvie De Moor;

Peter Ashworth, David Bailey, Nick Knight, Jean-Baptiste Mondino, Paolo Roversi, Sølve Sundsbø, Juergen Teller, Mario Testino, Roxanne Lowit;

Agencies: Art & Commerce, Contact Press, Rex, The Rappaport Agency, Getty Images;

Museums: The Norton Simon Museum, Manchester Art Gallery, Houghton Library at Harvard University;

The Lenders:
Kate Dooley (Giles Deacon),
Aitize Hanson, Jelka Music (Jean Paul Gaultier),
Charlotte Mercier, Soïzic Pfaff (Christian Dior Couture),
Gérald Chevalier & Juliette Iserin (John Galliano),
Alexandre Fiette, Danielle Luquet de Saint Gemain (Musée des Arts et Histoires, Genève),
Chigako Takeda (Comme des Garçons),
Carole Barlot (Thierry Mugler),
Cécile Chary (Montana archives),
Walter Van Beirendonck,
Laure Harivel (Montana),
Rafael Gomez (Vivienne Westwood),
Cornelia de Uphaugh, Maria Eisl (Stephen Jones),
Caroline Fabre Bazin (Azzedine Alaïa),
Scott Gray, Asa Larsson (Marc Jacobs)

&

Shirley Hex, Kim Bowen, Lee Sheldrick, Sibylle de St Phalle, MaryAnne McIntyre, Vicki Sarge, Dauphine de Jerphanion, Martin Margiela, Jacqueline Montana, Steven Robinson, Vanessa Bellanger, Bill Gaytten, Mariel Palacios, Adrian Joffe, Michael Roberts, Robert Forrest, Miles Chapman, Kerry Warn, Daniel McDowell

Patrick Dejaeger & Europal Group (Joke Roose & Ann Callens);
Bumble&Bumble (Tim Rush, Yves Van de Gucht);
Pascal Van Loenhout & team;
The Chocolate Line (Dominique Persoone);
ASAP Photographic Services (Charles Van der Heyden);
Eurostar (Saar Meylemans);
Hotel Les Nuits (Geoffrey Stampaert)

Media Partners: *Elle Belgium* & *Weekend Knack*

CATALOGUE

This catalogue is published in association with the exhibition 'Stephen Jones & The Accent of Fashion' (MoMu – Fashion Museum Province of Antwerp, September 8, 2010–February 13, 2011)

Authors
Hamish Bowles
Judith Clark
Oriole Cullen
Kaat Debo
John Galliano
Stephen Jones
Magdalene Keaney
Suzy Menkes

Graphic Design
Paul Boudens

Translation
Katy van Overzee
Mari Shields

Editing
Laura Potter
Karen Van Godtsenhoven

Image Research
Gemma Williams
Karen Van Godtsenhoven

With special thanks to
Andrew Bolton
Penny Martin
Dita Von Teese

Publisher
Lannoo Publishers, Tielt, Belgium

For the original edition:

Original title: *Stephen Jones & Het Accent op Mode*

www.lannoo.com

ISBN 978-185149-652-5

British Library Cataloguing-in-Publication Data: A catalogue record for this book is available from the British Library.

Printed in Belgium.

Published in England by ACC Editions, an imprint of the Antique Collectors' Club Ltd., Woodbridge, Suffolk.

www.antiquecollectorsclub.com